Writing Creative Non-Fiction

Determining the Form

A *Gylphi Limited* Book

First published in Great Britain in 2015
by Gylphi Limited

A CIP catalogue record for this book is available from the British Library.

ISBN 978-1-78024-024-4 (pbk)
ISBN 978-1-78024-025-1 (Kindle)
ISBN 978-1-78024-026-8 (EPUB)

Cover painting by Mark Brooks (http://www.markbrooks.net). Design and typesetting by Gylphi Limited. Printed in the UK by imprintdigital.com, Exeter.

Gylphi Limited
PO Box 993
Canterbury CT1 9EP, UK

Writing Creative Non-Fiction

Determining the Form

edited by

Laura Tansley and Micaela Maftei

Gylphi

Contents

Notes on Contributors

Jo Collinson Scott is a lecturer in commercial music at the University of the West of Scotland, where she helped develop the MA in Songwriting and Performance. She is also a professional songwriter and popular music performer working under the name Jo Mango. Under this guise she has co-written songs and collaborated on performances worldwide, with artists such as David Byrne, Teenage Fanclub, Vashti Bunyan and Devendra Banhart. Her AHRC-funded doctoral research at the University of Glasgow focused on the development of radical creative methodologies for analysing contemporary music. Jo's current research focuses on further developing these interdisciplinary and creative approaches to methodology and exploring their applicability to popular music with a focus on creativity studies, songwriting pedagogy and practice-based research contexts.

Rodge Glass is an author, editor, academic and critic. His books include *No Fireworks* (Faber, 2005), *Hope for Newborns* (Faber, 2008) and *Dougie's War* (Freight Books, 2010). His non-fiction work, *Alasdair Gray: A Secretary's Biography* (Bloomsbury, 2008), won a Somerset Maugham Award in 2009 and his latest novel, *Bring Me the Head of Ryan Giggs* (Serpent's Tail, 2012), was published as *Voglio la testa di Ryan Giggs* in Italy in 2014 (66thand2nd, Roma). His latest collection, *LoveSexTravelMusik: Stories for the Easyjet Generation* (Freight, 2013), was widely acclaimed and nominated for the International Frank O'Connor Award. He is a BA Programme Leader in Creative Writing at Edge Hill University in Lancashire, and in 2013/14 spent a year researching and writing his next novel, *Once a Great Leader,* in Latin America.

Rebecca Gordon Stewart holds a PhD from the University of Aberdeen. She was the Christopher Isherwood Foundation Fellow at the Huntington Library for 2009–10. Her work includes ‘I was obsessed by a complex terrors and longings connected with the idea of “War”’, in *First World War Studies;* ‘Christopher and Frank: Isherwood’s Representation of Father and Son in Kathleen and Frank’, in *A/B: Auto/Biography Studies;* ‘“How Can I Know What I Think Till I See What I Say?”: Christopher Isherwood, E. M. Forster, and Literary Self-Reflection’, in *Bloomsbury Influences.* She is currently researching the influence of D. H. Lawrence on Isherwood>s writing and is a lecturer at Bath Spa University and Oxford University’s academic exchange programme Advanced Studies in England.

Kapka Kassabova is a poet, novelist and travel writer. Her family emigrated from Bulgaria to New Zealand just after the fall of the Berlin Wall. *Street Without a Name* (2008) is her coming-of-age story of communist Bulgaria; it was short-listed for the Prix du livre européen and the Dolmann Travel Club Award. *Twelve Minutes of Love* (2011), short-listed for the Scottish Book Awards, is a story of Argentine tango, obsession and the search for home. Her novel *Villa Pacifica* (2011) is set in South America and her poetry collections are *Someone else’s life* (2003) and *Geography for the Lost* (2007). She is also a translator from Bulgarian and a regular contributor for the *Guardian, Intelligent Life,* and the *Scottish Review of Books.* After spending her late teens and twenties in New Zealand, Kapka moved to Scotland and now lives in the Scottish Highlands.

Katie Karnehm is Associate Professor of Writing and English at Indiana Wesleyan University in Marion, Indiana. She graduated from the University of St Andrews, Scotland, with a PhD in Creative Writing and an emphasis in creative nonfiction and poetry. She is working on a memoir of living and studying abroad in Europe. When she’s not writing essays, she’s walking her dogs and teaching yoga.

John I MacArtney completed his PhD in sociology at the London School of Economics in 2011. He is currently a post-doctoral research fellow at the University of Queensland, Australia. As well as his continuing interest in CAM and self-help, he is currently researching patient and carers' experiences of end of life and palliative care.

Micaela Maftei holds a PhD from the University of Glasgow. Her book *The Fiction of Autobiography: Reading and Writing Identity* was published with Bloomsbury in 2013 and her fiction has appeared online and in print in the UK and North America.

Rhiannon Marks is a lecturer in Welsh at the School of Welsh, Cardiff University. Her fields of specialism include literary theory and contemporary Welsh literature. She pursued her undergraduate studies at the University of Aberystwyth, completed an MSt degree at the University of Oxford and returned to Aberystwyth to write her PhD thesis on the work of Menna Elfyn. She has recently published her first academic volume with the University of Wales Press entitled *'Pe gallwn, mi luniwn lythyr': golwg ar waith Menna Elfyn* (2013), an experiment in epistolary criticism.

Helen Pleasance is a writer and researcher based in Manchester. The subjects she finds herself returning to are the relationship between photography and embodied identity and the histories and fictions of Manchester. Her research on Manchester may get turned into stories called 'From Peterloo to Primark' and 'Balotelli Stories and Other Stories'. She is completing a full-length memoir about the Moors Murders entitled 'Ghosts on the Hill'. She teaches Literature and Creative Writing for the Open University.

Elizabeth Reeder, originally from Chicago, now calls Scotland home. Her short writing has been widely published in journals and anthologies and has been broadcast on BBC Radio 4 as stories, drama, and abridgements. Her debut novel, *Ramshackle*, is published by Freight Books and was shortlisted for the 2013 Scottish Mortgage Investment Best First Book Award, the 2012 Saltire First Book Award, and longlisted for the 2013 Author's Club Best First book. Her second novel, *Fremont*, is published by Kohl Publishing. She teaches on and co-convenes Creative Writing at University of Glasgow.

Erin Soros of Vancouver, British Columbia, has published fiction and non-fiction in international journals and anthologies, and her stories have been aired on the CBC and BBC as recipients of the CBC Literary Award, the Commonwealth Prize for the Short Story, and as a finalist for the BBC Short Story Award. 'Still Water, B.C.' was recently a finalist for the UK's Costa Short Story Award. Erin also collaborates with other artists, studies philosophy, and teaches psychoanalysis, modern literature, and human rights. *Morning is Vertical,* a collection of prose and photographs that builds on the archival and oral history of logging communities on Canada's West Coast, is forthcoming from Rufus Books.

Laura Tansley's creative and critical writing has appeared in a variety of places including 'Short Fiction in Theory and Practice', 'New Writing', 'Versal' and 'The Island Review' (with Amy Mackelden), 'Kenyon Review Online' (with Micaela Maftei), 'New Writing Scotland' and 'NANO Fiction'. She lives and works in Glasgow.

Pathways to Determining Form

Laura Tansley and Micaela Maftei

The essays in this collection are remarkable for two reasons. First, they have exceeded expectations in a number of ways (style, originality, content and scope) throughout their development. Second, they form a record of a process, perhaps we might call it a journey, which began several years ago and will hopefully continue with every reader that comes across this book.

In June 2010, the editors organized and hosted a conference at the University of Glasgow. We were both studying there and we were, and continue to be, researchers and practitioners of a kind of writing that seems to reject its label, a label that is nevertheless employed for the purposes of advertising, marketing and editing, and recognized as a distinct genre (though how exactly this distinction manifests is contentious). During this time our interest in creative non-fiction was compounded by conversations with Creative Writing PhD students who were insistently separating the creative from the critical, despite the fact that there was no clear consensus on exactly how each category could be understood by themselves, their supervisors, lecturers or peers. We too were trying to understand what it meant to be undertaking a Creative Writing PhD, new as it was, unprecedented as it was; and all PhDs have an element of originality and sense of uncharted territory, but PhD programs in this subject area were still relatively new.

A Creative Writing thesis is often comprised of a creative piece and a critical discussion, complementary sections that strengthen each other. The specifics of the division (if there is one – postgraduate students have chosen to produce completely creative theses, which gives rise to the possibility of a completely critical Creative Writing thesis – it's more than likely that someone, somewhere, is participating in that project as we write this), can be established by the student, the supervisors and/or the department involved in the creation of the thesis. It also depends on where they study – different institutions have different guidelines and expectations, which will necessarily influence students' actions and decisions.

In our interactions with other Creative Writing postgraduates we experienced students and academics describing these sections in very different ways. For example, at a conference in 2009, a second-year Creative Writing PhD student suggested that 'the smart money was on getting the critical section out of the way in order to focus on the real writing'. The audience seemed to agree. Why, we wondered, were these students adamantly enjoying one kind of writing, and not the other? Why did they feel so differently about 'critical' writing when they obviously loved to write? It seemed they had relinquished their agency somehow when it came to the critical aspects of their PhD; that they were resigned (some more reluctantly than others) to write in a form that hindered their creative voices, understanding this as a condition of getting to later enjoy the kind of writing that seemed more important to them.

These experiences led to us wanting to speak to more writers in the hopes of discovering whether the creative processes involved in writing essays, critical analysis or any kind of non-fiction were really so far removed from the processes of writing fiction or poetry. And what about the writing itself: what kinds of understandings did writers have about the, sometimes inscrutable, line of demarcation used to separate non-fiction and fiction? How might an author define the writing they produced if it was neither non-fiction nor fiction? Or what if it was both? The outcome of these questions was 'Determining Form: Creative Non-fiction Journeys', a conference held at the University of Glasgow in June 2010.

As we discussed these issues and questions at the conference, we brought with us personal experiences of meeting with academics and authors from a variety of backgrounds: meetings that revealed a mutual understanding of the potential of creative non-fiction, of its complexities, of its power. And so we created an opportunity to meet individuals and learn about their explorative writings that could be said to be creative non-fiction, but were not held solely within communities of Literature or Creative Writing departments and programmes. Good writing, we believe, is desirable, and indeed essential, in a much wider range of fields: we were curious about the writing processes of any author, no matter what context or which field they were based in. The diversity of those people who presented papers as well as those in attendance created a dynamic mix of ideas and understandings, of complementing processes and products, of the responsibilities and choices made when choosing to write non-fiction.

We could include, here, a list of forms as a way to demonstrate what we understand creative non-fiction to be, but we would be falsely trying to define a genre that we know to be greater, and more complex, than the sum of its parts. Tracing its history would equally confine the genre to one specific understanding, and we are learning that creative non-fiction can, and does, have many interpretations. We know that the definition of what an essay is has been altered, confounded and conflated by John D'Agata's 2003 collection, *The Next American Essay,* although by choosing the term 'essay' to identify his writing, D'Agata is reaching back to Montagine and even earlier. The poster for the Glasgow conference explicitly referenced Truman Capote's *In Cold Blood,* a project called a 'non-fiction novel' by its author, and a key text in the discussion and history of non-fiction. We know that Vivian Gornick's discussion on the inclusion of fictional elements in her memoir *Fierce Attachments* at Goucher College in 2003 addressed in direct terms how some writers find it obvious and indeed necessary to use fiction techniques in non-fiction writing, as well as how appalling some readers, journalists and witnesses to her talk found this notion. This reaction demonstrates how many readers and writers hold to strict rules about what is permissible in (non-)fiction, but also that these rules very often clash. We found that each new example we discovered of writing usually classified as non-fiction which was testing and exploring what it meant to write truthfully seemed to lead to another example; from the furore over *A Million Little Pieces* in 2006, to the accusations of invasion of privacy surrounding author Åsne Seierstad's *The Bookseller of Kabul* in 2010, back to New Journalism in the 1970s, and then forward again and the retraction of 'Mike Daisey and the Apple Factory' by *This American Life* in 2012.[1] For us, the topic of creative non-fiction is reaching its critical mass, while a different history might suggest that this aspect of non-fiction has been bubbling away for half a century.

The essays included here are responses to, extensions of and new formulations of what we perceive to be a twenty-first century trend for re-evaluating creative non-fiction through experimentations with form and developing theories on craft. Jonathan Coe's 2003 *Like a Fiery Elephant* understands that in order to write effectively about the topic, the form must reflect the subject. In this way Coe's biography of B. S. Johnson, the innovative author of such experimental works as *The Unfortunates* (a novel presented in shuffled chapters, contained in a box and presented to the reader as an opportunity to read a text in whichever order they feel like), had to respond to this innovation, and sought to reflect the multiplicity of interpretations in Johnson's work by drawing attention to the role of the biographer: one man's story of another, and all the unknown that comes with that. David Shields' *Reality Hunger: A Manifesto*, both a diatribe and a joyful, playful exploration of the state of twenty-first century writing, essay and aphorism, again expresses the need for readers and writers to address multiplicity and interpretation as integral to art. A text that is full of unattributed quotes, Shields both demonstrates and discusses the power of collage and the multitude of texts that are at constant interplay in any piece of work, drawing attention to the notion of whose truth is present in any text. Alongside this, in a dedicated chapter and sprinkled throughout, Shields (2010: 116) discusses non-fiction: its potential, its boundless energy, and how the traditional novel is 'predictable, tired, contrived' and in need of some serious reinvigoration. It seems that he sees the limitations of the term 'non-fiction', but perhaps the possibilities as well. He writes, 'The roominess of the term *non-fiction*: an entire dresser labeled *nonsocks*' (Shields, 2010: 129, emphasis in the original). These two texts, out of many that have influenced the editors and authors of *Writing Creative Non-Fiction: Determining Form*, find reflections and responses in the pieces collected here, which simultaneously explore theory and practice, from both inside and outside of academia. Through these explorations authors are able to describe and discuss the effect these theories had on their craft as they perform it. We were in the fortunate position of witnessing this process occurring, and the effects this had our own scholarly practice and understanding of creative non-fiction has been great.

A key issue recurring in the discussions we had at the conference, imbibed by the essays collected here, has to do with writing non-fiction and the notion of 'truth'. Anyone who has paid even the slightest amount of attention to recent articles and books that test boundaries of truth-telling and honesty will know that this is a fascinating but controversial area. James Frey, Augusten Burroughs and now Lance Armstrong, the most obvious recent examples of non-fiction writers who falsified elements in their supposedly truthful books, have expanded discussions on the relationship between creative non-fiction and 'truth'.[2] The use of inverted commas highlights the hotly contested meaning and understanding of this word. The essays included here avoid simplistic or straightforward assumptions about the genre in relation to truth-telling and truthfulness, and so have become part of this continued exploration within creative non-fiction.

Unclear boundaries between fact and fiction can be freeing, allowing authors to tell stories using the structures, techniques and language of fiction, poetry and non-fiction, creating unique and personal testimony. In this way creative non-fiction can become a highly individual truth. Such testimony may be felt by the author to be truthful if not wholly factual.

In many ways, James Frey (2003) used such a defence when he argued that the embellishments in his account were there to 'serve the greater purpose of the book', a book in which he explored his personal understandings of addiction, if not his lived experience.

Though *Salon* called *A Million Little Pieces* 'a fierce and honourable work that refuses to glamorize the author's addiction or his thorny personality' (Bayard, 2003), subsequent events revealed that actually Frey did precisely that – created a 'skewed perception of himself' and wrote specifically from that persona (Frey, 2003). For many readers, the honour drained from his work very quickly when his deliberate falsifications were made clear. Subsequent editions now include various author's and publisher's notes: one from 2006 calls the book 'a subjective truth', while a bolded statement on the copyright page of a 2004 edition advises that 'The reader should not consider this book anything other than a work of literature'.

This example fails to bring us any closer to a conclusion, however. Fiction can be literature; so can creative non-fiction. Readers and writers alike will hopefully share our reluctance to get to any firm conclusion, but instead consider possibilities in writing and ask questions of presumptions and reactions to explore notions of truth. Undoubtedly Frey's articulation of questions about fact and fiction, as well as his answers, were profoundly affected by the sensational media storm surrounding the publication of his book. A writer coming from a rather different environment offers another way of looking at the borders between fact and fiction, though perhaps with no less radical answers. John D'Agata (2009), whose work repeatedly questions the form and effect of non-fiction, asks: 'Do we read non-fiction in order to receive information, or do we read it to experience art?'. Is it knowledge, art or some kind of mixture of these two that non-fiction creates? 2012's *The Lifespan of a Fact* draws out the exchanges between D'Agata and a fact-checker assigned to one of his essays, raising pertinent questions about fact, fiction, accuracy and how art can connect with any or all of these categories.

The ways in which readers respond to the exchanges between D'Agata and the fact-checker, and particularly the liberties D'Agata takes with specific and verifiable claims, cannot help but be affected by the assumptions and beliefs each reader brings with them to the reading. One anonymous reviewer at amazon.co.uk confessed to being 'foolish enough to believe the "facts" set out in the book. Turns out I was being improved with Art and Greater Truths. Oops' ('takingadayoff', 2012). Another describes the book as the fact-checker's 'increasingly exasperated attempt to hold D'Agata to a commonsensical standard of accuracy and D'Agata's increasingly defensive attempt to make Fingal feel primitive for believing in something so superannuated' (Lewis-Kraus, 2012). It takes no time at all to see that 'literature' is no explanation or guide at all in terms of finding a line between fact and fiction, nor is 'common sense'. These terms hardly apply on more than an individualized plane – one person's common sense is another's grave miscalculation.

This is why creative non-fiction offers such fertile ground for approaching questions that, despite being fundamental and basic, remain unanswerable. How do we know what happened? How can we tell what happened? These questions are simultaneously basic, almost simplistic in their phrasing, and yet fundamental, as so much about writing has to do with having a voice and telling a story, made subjective by the author/s. There is room for ambiguity in every story, and in the telling of every story.

The outcry over fiction discovered within non-fiction has much to do with the role stories play in our lives. Without them, we're rootless, we have no family, we come from nowhere and we are directionless. A life without a plot is merely an existence. To give depth, meaning and scope to our lives, we use a narrative arc. And because stories are never singular and never straightforward, our narrative arc will likely involve others' stories. Critic Paul John Eakin (2008: 2) suggests that, 'narrative is not merely *about* self, but is rather in some profound way a constituent part *of* self' (emphasis in original). Here he argues that stories are essential to who we are, to how we see the world, to how we understand ourselves. Stories are our lifeblood and more; they are our bodies, our relationships, our goals, our achievements. When Thomas King writes 'the truth about stories is that's all we are' (King, 2003: 2), he is clearly saying something that is perhaps not factually accurate (we are made of cells and skin and blood) but unquestionably true.

The issue of terminology is not the only debate here, but it is in some ways the most obvious. In *The Lifespan of a Fact*, D'Agata claims that the term non-fiction essentially means 'not art', since the word fiction is derived from the Latin 'fictio', which itself means 'to form, to shape, to arrange' – a fundamental activity in art (D'Agata cited in MacDonald, 2012). But changing the words doesn't really affect the whole discussion. In some ways this is because not everyone is in agreement about what to name things and why, which is why D'Agata's staff page on the University of Iowa website lists his research interests as 'Non-fiction Writing', but elsewhere he states, 'frankly I think that anyone who still identifies themself as a "non-fiction" writer isn't really someone I would take seriously' (von Arbin Ahlander, 2011).

Stories are tools, maps and valuable possessions. We use them and we need them to orient ourselves in the world, to present ourselves to others, and to interpret other individuals. John Sturrock points to this crucial function of storytelling when he claims that 'A human life can be brought to display a meaning only on condition of being turned into a story ... A life storied is a life made meaningful' (Sturrock, 1993: 20). Human relations are built on stories, from the most inane cocktail-party variety ('So what is it you do?'), which can be avoided if one is careful, to the most explosive and secret stories, told only to true intimates, after much time and trust.

Because stories are an important way to evaluate others, and because we use others' stories to measure our lives against, we take them seriously. Non-fiction suggests a means of performing the impossible – entering into someone else's story, someone else's world. Some non-fiction suggests the opportunity to closely witness or even experience alongside the writer, their story. If we use it to construct our own ideas about, for instance, experiencing divorce and raising a small child through a haze of alcoholism, as in Mary Karr's memoirs, or poverty in a slum in Ireland, like *Angela's Ashes,* or indeed substance abuse and extreme self-destruction, as in *A Million Little Pieces,* we can use the stories of those who have gone through those experiences. If we later find that the stories are not rooted in lived experience, thus making them no longer suitable for our purposes, we may get angry.

Writing non-fiction involves selection, pruning and editing, just like fiction. Joan Didion (2006b) sees the difference in the sense that, to her, writing fiction is like 'watercolours ... Every stroke you put down you have to go with'. Conversely, non-fiction is like 'sculpture', in the sense that she's crafting and shaping from what is already there (Didion, 2006b). Didion has spoken about the way writing is a way for her to learn what she thinks about something, to realize how she feels. Stories for her, are told 'in order to live', linking them with the life-giving capacity Eakin describes (Didion, 2006a: 185).

If we move back from energetic debate over what part of a story is true and what part isn't, we arrive in much more nuanced and complex, yet thrilling, territory. From another vantage point, we can perhaps more easily see that in most cases, there is no single version of what happened, and that a preoccupation with discovering just where information lies on either side of what must always be a more or less individually determined line stands in the way of accepting a piece of art on its own terms.

These moments, projects and authors remain significant to us and to our work, because they developed our understanding of creative non-fiction and they act as signposts along the way of what seems to be an ever-changing discussion and way of naming and reading. There are many other moments, publications and instances that could be, in a different timeline, as significant. But to complement the spirit of this collection, we will focus on our journey rather than trying to create a history. Contemporary theories of creative non-fiction are illustrated through discussions of the journeys that led to the production of writing, as well as the essays themselves, situating this collection in the dynamic position of being discursive as well as performative.

We're excited to be able to include essays in this collection that we first encountered as papers (or indeed as abstracts), some that weren't able to be presented on the day, as well as some that have changed significantly from their first appearance. What is apparent in all the essays collected here is their interest in scrutinizing and exploring the paths that led them to the places their writing created. The collection, therefore, is structured around recurring themes, including this notion of creative processes and how they affect the writing produced.

In keeping with our focus on a journey rather than a destination, working with some of our authors to produce essays informed and inspired by the conference has developed the ideas we were exposed to and deepened the connections between papers. Most obviously, the time between the conference and publication has opened a space for writers to reflect on how their essays, their ideas and they themselves have changed over time: a process that Elizabeth Reeder explicitly refers to in her piece. Likewise, Katie Karneham's contribution offers an examination of how her writing process for a particular project has changed since 2010, and how this change is negotiated and understood. Indeed, transforming her conference presentation into a thoughtful and probing essay has also created a narrative for the fundamental change that she is tracking in another writing project. As that project developed, so did her essay, resulting in a paper that is now very different from the presentation she gave, and yet irrevocably linked to it.

Our hope was to gather a group of writers curious about their own and others' processes, engaged in researching writing, writers or modes of expression, and writing extensively themselves. Their field of study or practice was of far less importance to us than their desire to analyse the writing they were doing, and their interest in how writing can challenge rather than enforce boundaries. Elizabeth Reeder's piece in particular explicitly challenges even the term creative non-fiction, suggesting that because the words employed are so laden with connotations and suggestions of fact, truth and creativity, readers' expectations of a piece of creative non-fiction are skewed, and may even be pre-determined. Reeder's essay puts forward a discussion that suggests that the term 'essay' frees writing from the boundaries that a term like creative non-fiction can create. And in this way she responds to the re-evaluation of texts, prompted by authors such as John D'Agata and the *The Next American Essay* collections, as they re/consider the definition and establish journeying as an integral aspect of 'essaying'.

Rhiannon Marks describes the unusual path she took during the writing of her thesis, and how this path was viewed by other students. She describes her cumulative, gradual approach, using her writing to track her progress as well as to display her growing awareness of what literary criticism and analysis could mean. Choosing to form her thesis around a series of un-sent letters to the Welsh poet Menna Elfyn had a profound effect on her understanding of the potential of critical writing and her understanding of Elfyn, as well as her understanding of her own writing process.

Jo Collinson Scott's essay also charts a journey. One of developing a mode of musical criticism that could reflect the aesthetic and theoretical aspects of music as well as the music itself. She recalls her experience of needing to create a form to suit the writing she wanted to produce after finding that the criticism surrounding pieces of music moved her more than the music itself ever could. This recollection extends the discussion of the importance of the process by introducing the idea of performativity in writing through examples of her schizoanalysis, as well as how writing can enact ideas as it expresses them.

Whether we tell stories and understand them as fiction or non-fiction, or whether we draw away from such classification, writers craft and shape writing – no experience exists on a flat plane; every instance, exchange, discussion, event is open to multiple interpretations and can be described in many ways, all of which are potentially truthful. Rodge Glass's essay balances his own authorial intentions, desires and hopes with those of his subject in his discussion of the experience of writing a biography. His contribution addresses the questions: which of the many versions of a man's life is the truest? And, how many forms can a biography take and still be truthful? His piece engages with the decisions a biographer must make, and the realization that as a biographer, his own story had to appear in the piece of writing. Every decision made by a biographer can be said to involve questions of truth and deception, and his articulation of biography as choosing one truth out of many possible truths, rather than somehow excavating and revealing the single true account of a life, alters how we often see these works.

In varied ways, all the authors in this text probe the notion of truth, understanding it as multiple, fragmentary, debateable. Rebecca Gordon's essay in particular finds ways of tracing these topics into fictional works that retain a strong autobiographical element: how does Christopher Isherwood's attempt at mythmaking relate to ideas of truth? Can we read his self-declared fictional works as nevertheless a way of gleaning information about his 'real' life? How do we determine his honesty in his writing? Rather than reading proclaimed non-fiction and discovering fictionalized elements, she reads fiction and considers how we might find lived experience and factual accuracy within it. While on some levels it seems a wider public grows increasingly incensed at 'discovering' deceit and untruth in works released as non-fiction, suggesting a strictly binary way of reading these works, the understandings of the fluidity of truth and fiction presented here offer new perspectives and approaches to the craft and theory of creative non-fiction.

Another related issue is the negotiation of authorial identity during the writing process: who are we when we write? And does the way we answer this question change when we write about ourselves? Much creative non-fiction is alluring for writers and readers because of the privileged place the writer can occupy. Both the creator, pulling the strings behind the scenes, and a character, featuring within the story being told, this form offers a dualistic way of reflecting on the effects of a moment in history. This is perhaps most obvious in memoir and other life writing, where the writer is both the character re/living an experience, and an author reflecting on that experience, but is also seen in journalism and biographies, where what the author learns about her/himself during the process of research and writing creates a wider truth, building a relationship with the subject of the piece and establishing a kind of conversation between subject, author and reader. Erin Soros' piece places the reader in a very particular position, simultaneously alienating us through the use of language, which also offers us an insider's perspective of a breakdown. As language breaks down, we lose our ability to understand, but nevertheless language leads us through the piece, to a place of understanding. We understand and cannot understand, which in turn helps us to understand.

She also engages with ideas of truth-telling in such writing: when selfhood is compromised in some way, how can we come to terms with multiple truths, and indeed multiple selves? How are you honest with yourself when the very ways in which you normally see yourself dissolve or disappear?

Kapka Kassabova's piece collapses these questions into the experience of a single individual: herself. And yet the issue is no less nuanced or complicated. When writing the past, across enormous cultural and temporal divides, how does one, how can one, stay true to the self at the time of writing as well as the self that one is writing about? She also engages with notions of physical space and place, and tracks the way our relationship to a place can be hugely informative in our process of self-making. Likewise, its absence – a sense of homelessness, or rootlessness, or the loss of a former home – can have similarly profound effects on how we see ourselves and where we can feel belonging.

John MacArtney's essay approaches these questions of identity and truth from a very different angle, but his discussion raises similar issues: how to stay truthful to a subject when a life-altering event necessarily changes the perspective from which one is writing. MacArtney's research had been filtered through the perspective of an outsider, and his process was irrevocably altered when he received a diagnosis that suddenly made him an insider. His essay considers the shift he had to make in his approach to his research in order to acknowledge his changed position in relation to his topic. His writing reveals how an event can create multiple new relationships to that which surrounds us (people, subjects, writing), why it felt important to alter his writing process to incorporate these new relationships, and how this affected his creative output. His work raises the question of whether, if he had chosen to ignore the way his role and status as a researcher had changed permanently (if this was even possible), his research and writing might have been (read as) untruthful.

The spectral elements of non-fiction haunt Helen Pleasance's contribution. She uses (and notes Hilary Mantel's use of) the motif of ghosts as an appropriate one for the genre. Former versions of events, other accounts, identities now muted or silenced through death, haunt these writings, and must be acknowledged and incorporated. The ghostliness is the past and its infinite interpretability; it is the various (perhaps contradicting) textual strategies and their use, which floats through a text to create an illusion, an echo of something unattainable, lost as it is in time. Pleasance describes the way mythological narrations can become history, how we attempt to capture reality in writing, though this remains impossible. The past cannot be captured because there is no past to capture, only multiple pasts instead. And all versions will involve the current speaker and their existing identity, which subsequently changes each utterance of the past. Pleasance's own experience of writing memoir is influenced by and influences her understanding of the spectral engagement with history, as she attempts to understand her father's role in the historical narrative of the Moors Murders. Her father's 'real' identity, with which she had a particular relationship, becomes diffuse and slippery as she engages with other versions of his self and his story; his death complicates this even further, irrevocably changing their relationship, as well as his role within others' interpretations of the Moors Murders narrative(s).

Pleasance's essay, like many of the other essays in this collection, expresses and critiques the significance of the author recognizing their own position, reflecting on this and moving forward accordingly. The author of creative non-fiction is often expected to be able to recreate reality, to deal with, or even to access, a singular truth, but the author, like any human, is not an automaton remotely tasked with capturing a life or an event. Christopher Isherwood (1999: 243) writes, 'I am a camera with its shutter open, quite passive, recording, not thinking ... Some day, all this [that the camera records] will have to be developed, carefully printed, fixed'. This quote is something that writers, critics and editors return to again and again because it draws attention to their role in the creative process. For an author, editor or critic, the choice of how to approach their subject is as intrinsic as the writing itself to creating a piece of work. It involves a process of understanding how an author influences their subject. The passivity that Isherwood describes here might relate to a particular aspect of the creative process – inspiration perhaps, and the indescribable way it can come over a writer – but this passivity cannot persist. If the eye is a camera, then what is seen through the lens is congruously linked with the mind and body behind it. As the work is 'developed', the author, editor or critic is at once inside and outside of the text they are constructing, and the essays in this collection explore the ways in which this is coordinated, redressed and complicated. There may be a moment when this writing is 'fixed', but that moment passes instantaneously, never to be recovered, and the writing becomes once more vulnerable to, open to, and available for, interpretations.

At the outset of this introduction we mentioned a comment offered by a Creative Writing PhD student at a conference. It seems only prudent now to remind the reader of the truth of this recreation of a comment, but that it is just that: a recreation. It is not the original comment. We did not record the presentation that featured the sentence that sparked the idea for the conference that led to this collection. We're not sure that the ordering of the words employed here is the same as the original utterance, but it doesn't make it any less true, significant or vital here, as it is presented to you. We have the confidence to approach the subject of truth here because of the company we keep: insightful and remarkable essays which have taught us much about the genre, subject, form – however you'd like to consider it – of creative non-fiction, and we're pleased to be able to present them in this unique collection. The publication of writing is one stage in hopefully a long life; and as pleased as we are to be able to share this writing with a wider audience, we are just as excited to track the changing relationship readers have with the text(s), and hopefully witness ways in which different interpretations and contextualizations can influence published, and therefore 'fixed', writing.

The Editors

Notes

1 We are, of course, confined to a certain amount of space in this introduction but if the reader is so inclined, more information on the case verdict of *The Bookseller of Kabul* can be found here: http://www.guardian.co.uk/theguardian/2010/jul/31/bookseller-of-kabul-interview-asne-seierstad; a transcript of Oprah Winfrey's interview with James Frey dis-

cussing *A Million Little Pieces* can be found here: http://www.oprah.com/oprahshow/Oprahs-Questions-for-James; and the retraction statement by Ira Glass on behalf of *This American Life* regarding 'Mike Daisey and the Apple Factory' can be found here: http://www.thisamericanlife.org/blog/2012/03/retracting-mr-daisey-and-the-apple-factory.

2 James Frey's *A Million Little Pieces*, Augsten Burroughs' *Running with Scissors* and Lance Armstrong's *It's Not About the Bike* are the texts we are referring to here.

References

Armstrong, Lance (2001) *It's Not About the Bike: My Journey Back to Life*. London: Yellow Jersey.

Bayard, Louis (2003) 'The Sound Bite and the Fury' (19 April) accessed 12 August 2013, http://www.salon.com/2003/04/19/frey/

Burroughs, Augusten (2004) *Running With Scissors*. London: Atlantic Books.

Coe, Jonathan (2005) *Like a Fiery Elephant: The Story of B. S. Johnson*. London: Picador.

D'Agata, John (2009) *The Lost Origins of the Essay*. St Paul: Greywolf Press.

And Jim Fingal (2012) *The Lifespan of a Fact*. New York: W. W. Norton and Company.

Didion, Joan (2006a) *We Tell Ourselves Stories in Order to Live: Collected Non-fiction*. London: Alfred A. Knopf.

Didion, Joan (2006b) 'The Art of Nonfiction No.1', *The Paris Review*, interviewed by Hilton Als, accessed 12 August 2013, http://www.theparisreview.org/interviews/5601/the-art-of-non-fiction-no-1-joan-didion

Eakin, Paul John (2008) *Living Autobiographically: How We Create Identity in Narrative*. New York: Cornell University Press.

Frey, James (2003) *A Million Little Pieces*. New York: Random House.

Hill, Amelia (2010) 'Bookseller of Kabul author Åsne Seierstad: "It's not possible to write a neutral story"', *Guardian* (31 July), accessed 12 August 2013, http://www.guardian.co.uk/theguardian/2010/jul/31/bookseller-of-kabul-interview-asne-seierstad

Isherwood, Christopher (1999) *The Berlin Novels*. London: Minerva.

King, Thomas (2003) *The Truth About Stories: A Native Narrative*. Toronto: House of Anansi Press.

Lewis-Kraus, Gideon (2012) "The Fact-Checker Versus the Fabulist." *New York Times*

Magazine, 21 February, accessed 12 August 2013, http://www.nytimes.com/2012/02/26/magazine/the-fact-checker-versus-the-fabulist.html?pagewanted=all&_r=0

MacDonald, Jennifer B. (2012) 'In the Details', *New York Times* (21 February), accessed 12 August 2013, http://www.nytimes.com/2012/02/26/books/review/the-lifespan-of-a-fact-by-john-dagata-and-jim-fingal.html?pagewanted=all&_r=0

Oprah.com (2006) 'Oprah's Questions for James', accessed 12 August 2013, http://www.oprah.com/oprahshow/Oprahs-Questions-for-James

Shields, David (2010) *Reality Hunger: A Manifesto*. London: Hamish Hamilton.

Sturrock, J. (1993) *The Language of Autobiography: Studies in the first person singular*. Cambridge: Cambridge University Press.

'takingadayoff' (2012) Amazon.co.uk (12 April), accessed 12 August 2013, http://www.amazon.co.uk/The-Lifespan-Fact-John-Dagata/dp/0393340732/ref=sr_1_1?ie=UTF8&qid=1360831682&sr=8–1

This American Life (2012) 'Retracting Mr Daisey and the Apple Factory' (16 March), accessed 12 August 2013, http://www.thisamericanlife.org/blog/2012/03/retracting-mr-daisey-and-the-apple-factory

von Arbin Ahlander, Astri (2011) Interview with John D'Agata, *The Days of Yore* (22 February), accessed 12 August 2013, http://www.thedaysofyore.com/john_dagata/

A Bulgarian Journey

Kapka Kassabova

In 2006, the editor of a London publisher said to me: 'Kapka, why don't write a book about Bulgaria – your communist childhood, and what's happened to the country since the fall of the Berlin Wall? You know, the Bulgarian story.'

My first reaction was: What? Nobody even knows where or what Bulgaria is. Well, exactly, she said.

At first, this appeared to be an impossible task, for several reasons.

One reason was the problem of how to rescue an entire country from an entrenched, persistent, and dated cliché.

When I first arrived in Britain as a teenager in 1990, my English consisted of whatever words I had picked up from listening to the Beatles and the German rock band The Scorpions. But even my rudimentary English was enough to make sense of the quiz I found in an English tabloid newspaper. One of the quiz questions was:

Bulgaria is (a) a character in a children's story; (b) a Soviet republic; (c) a country in south-east Europe, or (d) a wild river in Mexico.

Some British perceptions have changed since then; others have remained. And the same can be said about Bulgaria itself, a country where the totalitarian gerontocracy fell and their children took over with the money their fathers and grandfathers had been stealing from the country for half a century. From the Wild East, Bulgaria turned overnight into the Wild West.

In Britain, there still prevails an image of Bulgaria as a cheap and nasty place, mostly associated with cheap beer, cheap skiing, cheap sea-side resorts, cheap property, cheap sex, and nasty poisoned-tip umbrella murders. Skiing in Bulgaria has been described by the *Guardian* as 'crazily, undeniably, ridiculously cheap', and travel articles about the country still bear headings like 'I'm starting to love this dirty town'.

We could say that a national cliché is not only the product of ignorance, but also the extent to which the collective imagination has ran out of ideas. Ultimately, the side-effect of cultural cliché is to dehumanize places and people. I wanted to humanize a place and a people.

Reason two: I felt disconnected from my subject because I had spent sixteen years deliberately disconnecting myself from my home country, in order to survive elsewhere and forge a new, 'global soul' identity for myself. I therefore felt that I didn't have a story to tell. This changed suddenly when three years ago, I found myself cheerfully backpacking around Bulgaria for two months, in an attempt to write a new travel guide for the Globetrotter Travel Guides. I wanted this to be an uncomplicated, straightforward experience, like writing any other travel guide. I had done it in India, why not Bulgaria?

The journey had all the trauma and catharsis of a return.

At times, during my tour of Bulgaria, I felt as if I had slipped back in time, especially when I found myself staying in dated, brown Communist-era hotels and eating reheated food in forlorn restaurants where the waitress seemed to have popped out of the mid-1980s, with blue eye make-up and a bored expression.

In other words, I discovered that travelling simply in the present tense is impossible in Bulgaria. In some places, travel necessarily involves time-travel. The German ethnographer Felix Kanitz had said, back in the 1800s: 'A journey through Bulgaria is marked at each turn by the catacombs of expired peoples and eras' (Kanitz, 1882).

This is how the embarrassed tears of remembrance and loss came about for me – as I found myself simultaneously inside the scenes and smells of my childhood, *and* inside the lost world of Communism's twilight.

So, this uneasy reconnection with my former homeland began with a factual travel guide, passed through an unsentimental sentimental journey, and ended with a bittersweet memoir which I called *Street Without a Name,* because the Sofia street where I'd grown up didn't have a name. Today, in a neat twist, which proves that fiction cannot compete with fact, it is called Resurrection Street.

I was only able to re-enter the Bulgarian story by reconnecting with my own story. And that meant my own feelings, which had been filed away since 1990 when I'd emigrated from the country with my family. The only authentic, sincere way of beginning to tell the Bulgarian story was to tell *my* story of growing up and coming of age in the last decade and a half of the Cold War; my story of scurrying to the coveted West in the chipped shadow of the fallen Berlin Wall; and my story of returning sixteen years later as someone else in someone else's country.

And so the book turned out as a tale of two halves. In the first half, a child grows up in an oppressive but strangely entertaining environment that suddenly collapses. In the second, the grown-up child carries out her 'dream of glorious return' to the land of her past.

In the middle is the abyss of emigration and life elsewhere. One reader said to me that she felt as if at the end of part one, the protagonists – me and my family – fall off a cliff. And that's exactly how emigration is.

In part one, in other words, I tell the story of the last communist childhood, as it was lived, more or less, by my generation of ordinary kids from the Eastern bloc. We came of age just as the Berlin Wall came down.

Certain collective stories are too painful to be rendered directly – it is like staring at the sun, it blinds you. Both geographical and temporal distance is needed, so that the light can be refracted, and you can begin to find a tone in which to tell this story coherently.

Eva Hoffman in *Letters of Transit* observes that 'the great advantage, for a writer, of exile, the compensation for the loss, is that it gives you a perspective, a vantage point. Loss is a magical preservative.' (Hoffman, 1997).

And so in the pickle of memory, seasoned by the actual physical journey, there appeared a story. The narrative of part one – the childhood memoir – became, instinctively and organically, a conversation between the child (standing by her grandparents' Skoda in 1976) and the traveller, the grown up.

Non-fiction stories of course have one very particular duty: the duty of truth. Every writer, like every child, has a streak of pure ruthlessness in them, because their first vow is not to any one person, not even to themselves, but to the story, and therefore to the truth their story illuminates. I am not talking about facts here, but about the truth of a time and place that emerges, like a face in the water, as you sail back in time.

Another duty the memoir has is to avoid its own cliché of sentimentality, and that is only possible if the sharpness of the immediate experience is recreated – in this case, it was a child's experience. And so the child grows up and returns to someone else's country. This ceases to be metaphorical and becomes quite literal with places like Bulgaria, which have gone through cataclysmic historical and political changes. The lost world of Communism (and this is the title of a series of BBC documentaries about the Eastern Bloc) cannot be found anywhere anymore, except in our memories. Vesna Goldsworthy in *Chernobyl Strawberries* talks about this: 'The world I left behind, and which I am now revisiting from the distance of twenty years and well over a thousand miles, was that of Yugoslavia in the throes of the big communist experiment. Yugoslavia no longer exists, not even as a name' (Goldsworthy, 2005: 2).

And so in the second part of Street, I revisit, literally and close-up, the country that used to be mine. In *Goodbye to Berlin*, Christopher Isherwood, an outsider in a foreign city, adopted the perspective of 'a camera with its shutter open, quite passive, recording, not thinking.' (Isherwood, 1939: 13). My case was different. Travelling around the country where you grew up, lost some of your virginity and a few of your illusions, acquired some lasting neuroses, and then left in a hateful mood, is a schizoid experience. You are at once an outsider to the present and an insider of the past, or perhaps the other way around, hence the schizoid split.

In any case, the insider is revisiting, and it is the emotional charge and urgency of that re-visitation (and I use the ghostly word re-visitation deliberately) that haunts the story with an emotional urgency. The outsider, on the other hand, is *just visiting*, and has enough distance to see the universal in the particular, and the laughter in the tears.

And what enabled the insider and the outsider to merge into one single narrative persona was the very *ingloriousness* of the glorious return that Salman Rushdie has talked about. The return is always inglorious, and that gives us the comedy, the sadness, the pity, and if we are lucky, the redemption of return. The opening line to my journey across modern Bulgaria comes from an unnamed Yugoslav child who was recorded saying in the 1990s, 'I love my country. Because it's small and I feel sorry for it.'

I would like to finish with something Joyce Carol Oates has said: 'For most novelists, the art of writing might be defined as the use to which we put our homesickness.' This is quite literally true for journeys that are rooted in a landscape. Any journey through time-space activates the homesickness at the heart of the writer–traveller, and ultimately of the reader. My hope in writing *Street Without a Name* in the most unsentimental way possible was not just to tell the Bulgarian story, but to open up a couple of broader questions: can we go back to the land of childhood, and at what price? With the hope that each reader wherever they were as a child will find their own answers.

References

Goldsworthy, V. (2005) *Chernobyl Strawberries*. London: Atlantic Books.

Hoffman, E. (1997) 'The New Nomads', in A. Aciman (ed.) *Letters of Transit*. New York: The New Press.

Isherwood, C. (1939) *Goodbye to Berlin*. London: Vintage.

Kanitz, F. (1882) *Donau-Bulgarien und der Balkan*, three volumes. Leipzig: Salzwasser-Verlag.

At the Will of Our Stories

John I MacArtney

> Stories we tell ourselves about what is happening to us are dangerous because they are powerful. Stories come to us from many sources; some we seek, many happen without our notice, others impose themselves on our lives. We have to choose carefully which stories to live with, which to use to answer the question of what is happening to us. (Frank, 1991/2002: 81)

When I started my research into people's experiences of cancer and use of Complementary and Alternative Medicine (CAM) and self-help, I had a not unusual claim to a personal experience of the disease; during the 1990s I had watched my mother 'battle' and 'survive' cancer. Indeed it was her experience that was brought to mind when I read Carlos Novas and Nikloas Rose's (2000) paper on somatic individuality, which in turn started my initial ruminations that manifested into my doctoral research. That project, as PhD research projects do, morphed and changed. But in February 2009 I was faced with becoming my own research subject. My discovery of a lump, later confirmed as testicular cancer, substantially altered my position in relation to my research in a way few ever get to experience.

It was in early spring 2009 when I found myself in front of a surgeon who had delivered the news that, not only did she strongly suspect the worst for this lump, but I would be needing to return as a day surgical case the next morning. The surgery passed without incident and my partner, family and friends supported me in the following weeks as I recovered. However, after blood tests and CT scans I still did not know whether the lump was malignant or not, as the usual markers were not present. It was only a few weeks later, when the biopsy results returned, that the differential diagnosis was confirmed as cancer.

As a result of this diagnosis, I took the decision to have some exploratory surgery to see if the cancer had spread to my lymph nodes. Unfortunately an unforeseeable complication left me with a slow internal bleed. In the hours and days after surgery my condition deteriorated until a further round of surgery located and stopped the offending blood vessel. But my recovery was not yet assured. As I came round my right lung partially collapsed, leading me to spend a night in the Intensive Care Unit (ICU), with all the drama and technological intervention that involved. Given all this, I found, to my great surprise, that I could return home within a few short days of going back to the surgical ward.

The hope for the second surgery had been that it would tell me whether or not the cancer had spread and, if so, it would make the decision about chemotherapy an easier one to make. And it did: the biopsy results showed that the cancer had spread and so within three weeks of my eventful trips to theatre I was again lying on a hospital bed. This time the treatment was to have two blasts of chemotherapy, eight days apart. The cumulative effect of all this treatment was starting to take its toll. I was exhausted from my previous treatments, and within a week of the last chemotherapy I was due to move out of my flat. Again I was to rely on the strength of my partner, family and friends to get me through, which largely consisted of carefully depositing me at my partner's parents' home in the South England countryside to convalesce. Biomedicine had declared that it had done all it could for me, for the time being, so all I had to do was recover from its interventions and wait to see what happened. The waiting for cancer's return drifted comfortably into preparing for my return to my previous life. These days were occupied with dozing in the shade and long walks with the family dog in the late summer sun. By early autumn I was mentally and physically fit enough to return to everything I had dropped by the wayside in the previous months, dust it down and ask myself, what was it that I was doing again?

But when I returned to my research the question that immediately became apparent was, how would I account for this change in position within the research itself? With half the interviews conducted as a concerned 'outsider', I found I could not now re-write the voice of the thesis as though I had always been an 'insider'. Furthermore, to do so would lose an interesting point of contrast for the research. I had a highly unusual opportunity to document in real time a patient's experience of cancer, as a sociologist who already had a specific interest in the narratives of people who have, or have had, cancer and who use CAM. What was opening up to me was an opportunity to explore the formations of my subjectification, as a subject within my subjectivity.

So the question emerged, how to account for 'my account'? This question was one that was not just directed at making sure that I conveyed an effective story of my cancer, and not just the clinical facts, but it also denotes my unusual position. Here it is useful to introduce Harrington's (2008: 24–5) distinction between stories and narratives: stories are living, local and specific, and narratives are described as templates. Put another way, narratives provide the tropes and plotlines that import the specific stories that are heard, read or seen in action. In these terms, I was particularly concerned not to let my analytical story dominate those of the interviewees who had given their time to my research. However, it was evident that I would share experiences and narratives from the field, many of which I would be unaware of until I had engaged my story in further reflection and analysis.

While I considered what to do, I re-read Arthur Frank's book *At the Will of the Body*. Those who know this book will see that it is an obvious choice; he too is a sociologist of health and illness who had testicular cancer. What followed in my reflections largely became a conversation with his story and his larger corpus of work, a conversation that explored an insider/outsider dialogue, which is also the concern of the collection of essays in this book. My attention was specifically drawn to considering how I could acknowledge Frank's point in the epigraph. My story would be affected by all those narratives and experiences I had become aware of during my research, but I should not let the *analysis* become either an affirmation of my experiences, where the voices of those that I interviewed are indistinguishable from mine, or an abstracted account unable to situate the difference my experience brought to the analysis.

Therefore, with these two concerns in mind I first sought to write an account of 'My Cancer'. I drew together the thoughts and reflections that I had jotted down in my journal and, in particular, in the emails to my friends and family. My account drew heavily from these emails as much of the sense making happened in the writing of them. The writing of emails to people very close to me became my opportunity to edit and present what was happening to me.

When I looked at my emails it was possible to find that each email had a sense of a beginning and each had a feeling of its place. It was only later that it was possible to discern whether this was near the beginning, middle or end of My Cancer story. The chaotic anti-narrative present in the midst of ongoing events (Frank, 1995) was therefore somewhat strategically managed. This was often with the use of and referral to regurgitated medical language, which Frank might reason barely qualified them as narratives. But I found them to be like a clunky daytime soap opera, where the end point was unknown, yet there was a distinctive voice that was choosing what to regurgitate and, more importantly, how it was presented – the tone and affect conveyed allow the reader to know it was a story that they were being told. I could be sure of this, as one or two emails in response commented on how well I presented my story of My Cancer.

I also continued to write in my journal after my treatment had finished, and the reflections from that formed a second part of my story. At first writing these reflections was not something that I was particularly keen to do; I was happy that I had survived and, in the main, done so in a way that had minimised cancer's effects upon my loved ones and myself. But the push to reflect came from the need to understand My Cancer story in the face of all those stories that I knew before I was ill, and would hear as I progressed with my research.

What I needed to consider and examine were my experiences in light of the germinating structure that I had placed down for my PhD thesis, just before I had to stop work on it. I felt it was important for me to recognize the narratives and 'blind spots' in my own experiences before I continued to analyse those of my interviewees. However, when writing I sought to avoid doing this as part of a thematic analysis. I did not want to use my provisional analysis of my interviewees as a framework for my own story. At the same time it would be quite impossible not to be affected by the stories I had heard, the books I had read and the opinions I was developing, when I was writing my reflections. The problem this presented could not be easily overcome by pretensions to an objective method, yet I also wished to resist an auto-analysis that was comprehensible only in its own terms. So instead of attempting to ignore or eliminate any 'bias', writing my story of My Cancer became the instigator of owning that problem, of providing an 'honest' account (Back, 2007: 19).

In practice this meant putting my reflections and emails into a chronological framework and lightly editing them to form a story of My Cancer. But the process of doing this initiated a further process of reflection and analysis, as I started to write about my concerns upon returning to my research. The following section provides a digest of these musings, which sought to struggle with the multitude of expectations and experiences from the field of research, my personal experience, my private life and my academic aspirations.

* * *

> The responsibility of the ill, then, is not to get well but to express their illness well. And the two have nothing to do with each other... I believe that those who express their illness live their lives fully to the end of the illness. For me this is enough – it has to be enough. (Frank, 1991/2002: 127)

My ongoing wellness was not the end of My Cancer story. By this I mean two things: first, it may just be a hiatus for the disease. Second, I also had a serious period of illness to reflect upon. And one of the first things that I reflected upon was my experience of my body. In particular, I was always interested in the various ways that cancer was perceived and experienced in its relation to the body in the stories I read. Arthur Frank, in *At the Will of the Body*, described his mother-in-law's experience of cancer as 'abstracted', as she was fortunate to be operated on before she felt the pain that cancer can cause. This, compared to the 'reality' of his crippling experience, might be seen to set the two ends of experiencing the thing that is cancer. But this spectrum seems misplaced for my experiences. Cancer was a definite experience, but often with a non-specific object that was allowed to morph and excite my body and mind in a variety of different ways.

For example, after the small but 'aggressive' lump was removed, it was evident that we were chasing a stealth cancer, as I referred to it to my emails. It did not show up on any blood tests or CT scans. But that did not mean it was not still there. Of course, I could wait for it to come knocking in my body; await the lumps, bumps and pains to appear. Or we could get closer, beyond my blood and into the cells of my lymphatic system, to see if we could see it in a biopsy. The reality, though microscopic, was physically real. It did not have to cripple me in bodily pain for me to feel its presence. But this is not an abstract account of cancer via the proxy of medical intervention, as for Frank's mother-in-law. This was a molecular-reality, available on a different spectrum, at a different scale that is made available through the technology of the microscope, but experienced through a different language of the body (Novas and Rose, 2000).

But it was in a search for a language of the body that my account found echoes with Frank's and those of my interviewees. Frank's account includes a sense of 'wonder' at the body. At different times I had a similar intense awareness of my body – such as in the days after I left the ICU and my body seemed to recover exponentially, from death's door to walking wounded in a matter of days. As Frank notes, these are experiences that use language in a way that goes further than biomedicine's disease language will allow. But where does that take us? 'Wonder' is one such attempt to forge a language of illness. It is something that seeks to identify something more than mind–body conceptualizations have access to. It also has echoes of the language of the holistic body that are present in the complementary medicine field. This language of the (ill) body had been at the forefront of my work before I was ill and would continue to be after I returned.

Having spent so much time reading complementary literature, attending the centres, talks, open-days and fairs, it would be strange if the narratives within it had not influenced my story. But there are two areas that I found, when I reflected on my cancer, that I did not seem to share with my interviewees – in my initial analysis at least. First, to paraphrase the literature, the place the cancer has in the person's life. Often this is referred to as a 'turning point' (cf. LeShan, 1990); that is, it is some form of springboard to changes taking place in their life. The second aspect refers to the 'spiritual' dimension, or the 'deeper' contemplations that people have about life.

Looking at my own thoughts in my emails and journal, I saw that my initial reaction had been to fail to spot any significant changes or transformations in my life. But this, I considered, was more because I had been contemplating what it is to have cancer, or be at a higher risk of cancer, for many years now. For a long time, since my later teenage years, I considered myself to be at a high risk of bowel cancer, due to the family history on my mother's side. For many years I had slowly adapted my lifestyle to reduce my risks, mainly though adapting my diet. However, in 2007, I tested negatively for the familial bowel cancer gene. But instead of reverting to a less restricted diet I continued with it. It would seem that this was for two reasons: habit was certainly one; second, the diet I had was generally considered to be a 'health conscious' one. So there was no major turning point, more the gradual movement, all of which happened before My Cancer. All that had happened afterwards seemed to continue that gradual trajectory.

So what of the spiritual aspect? It was evident that along with the changes to my diet I had a history of reflecting on my attitude to life. Nonetheless, My Cancer story contained evidence of situating my life in the world around me. For example, immediately after my differential diagnosis I sat in a square outside the commercial centre of London. As I enjoyed the sun on my face I felt my life slow to a freeze-frame pace, while all around me the lunchtime rush commenced. Similarly, at various times while waiting for my second surgery, while I was effectively 'well', I walked around the city, taking time to be within, but somehow not a part of, the hustle and bustle of city life. Whereas the times I later spent recuperating in the countryside provided a geological backdrop to my increasing fitness, as I explored the rural landscape around me.

One walk found me sitting on top of a hill, overlooking the vale below, where, as I enjoyed the fields full of summer colours and volume, I felt a deep joy for life. Yet I was also aware of time passing, sometimes like a large grandfather clock in a dank and empty Victorian room. I had been off work for longer than at any point since I started a paper round at thirteen-years old. This in itself was a strange experience. As Frank notes, being ill 'releases' you from these 'productive' duties, but can leave you feeling cast aside. Nevertheless, along with these worries, this clock also provided a certain freedom. But I always felt that it was a freedom on loan. I knew I could not spend all the time I had like this, on top of a hill. I could only liken this paradoxical state to the feeling often experienced towards the end of a two-week holiday, when you *just* start to feel relaxed and settled, but when you realize that you will be back at work in a few short days. At that moment of realization, this freedom was like being gifted with a third week. But on other days, it was like living that realization on that penultimate day, over and over again.

Polyphonic Experiences: My 'Companion illness' and Analytical Guide

Frank (2010), borrowing from Donna Haraway's 'companion species', describes people's relations to stories as 'companion stories' using two parallels: first, he notes how companions shape each other in their progressive coevolution; and second, how companions generally take good care of each other, 'although 'taking care' always involves each shaping the other' (Frank, 2010: 43). In both instances, Frank notes, the companion enables the other to be. What was evident to me was that I now had two important companions: the embodied and ever present experience of My Cancer that was what I call a 'companion illness', and the epistemological concerns that arose whenever I engaged my experiences in the field and that constituted my 'analytical guides'. The dialogue between these two forms of experiencing the field then became a central concern of my reflections on my subjectification.

What was particularly troublesome to me after I returned to my research was the realization that what had become my companion illness was an experience that could be summarized as 'remission-as-normality', i.e. being somewhere between 'illness-as-normality' (Frank, 2010: 121) and being a member of the 'remission society' (Frank, 1995: 8). As I spent time in various self-help and CAM groups I became aware of this experience of remission-as-normality that I had started to tentatively wear. It was, as Frank (1995: 32) might put it, developing into a narrative of 'meta-control' that allowed me to 'pass' (Goffman, 1963/1990). It covered for the anxiety that my reality was really a faux-remission. My concern upon re-entering the field was that my companion illness of remission-as-normality would be challenged or even destroyed; but what I found was a recognition that most of us in the groups carried some sort of dual cancer passport that allowed us to be both 'ill' and 'well' (Sontag, 1979/2009).

However, 'remission-as-normality' would be unacceptable as an analytical account to many researchers in the field. This is because, as Frank (2010) describes, a 'good story', understood as one that engages people's imagination, holds them in suspense and calls for interpretation, is not always a 'good story' in terms of encouraging 'goodness'. Social science tends to focus on the former of these two understandings of a good story, Frank argues, and often serves to perpetuate those individuals or groups under analysis. In order to engage the latter Frank draws on Rabinow and Rose's (2003) 'practice of critique': a critique that does not seek to argue from a standpoint of what *should* count as good, but rather highlights what the cost is for saying that something is good in the way that it is conceived or enacted. This is not a 'revelatory' practice; rather it is the situating of the analytical practice as a process that is continually producing the field it seeks to study.

Returning to my problem: for me, asserting the socio-linguistic competence of 'remission-as-normality' as a companion illness was sufficient to demonstrate that My Cancer was a good (well-told) story that enabled me to 'be' in most spheres of life. However, in the production of research such assumptions were problematic, as by asking 'what are the analytical costs of my story?' I found My Cancer assumptions to be ethically loaded. Indeed, My Cancer story was somewhat a self-contradictory attempt to refuse cancer as a companion illness at all. Through this refusal, I allowed space for, but did not give form to, the other companion stories that formed and enabled me. But it was having cancer as a companion illness to my analytical guides that initiated my attitude to move away from being caught within either compelling story. As Frank argues, the polyphony of narratives is part of what makes stories ethical; the beginning of thinking about stories is placing one with another or more. This is part of, Frank (2010: 149) argues, 'living well with stories'.

For Frank, being caught up in, and thinking 'with', a story allows the analyst to learn from it and come to understand how the story can engage people, which then enhances the interpretive possibilities of his or her analysis. But Frank also notes that in order to avoid missing what the story excludes, one must eventually come to think analytically 'about' stories. But this is not a strict dichotomy, as there is no 'outside' of stories. This 'thinking about' is never purified or abstracted. Nor is it seeking 'to go back to' a story, as each re-telling – even in the context of a research thesis – is another telling and the production of another story. But the process of telling and re-telling has other advantages. Frank argues that one must learn to think with other stories in order to think about a given story in a better way. For Frank, having two stories or more makes an important ethical difference, as the dialogue they instigate is the start of learning to 'think about'. This leads Frank to argue that good storytellers 'bring in more stories'. Indeed, what they need to do is allow stories to bring in other stories themselves, as Frank argues this is what 'good' stories do anyway.

When I started my research, the story I brought with me was about a researcher who had a familial experience of cancer and complementary therapies in his life. As noted, my mother's cancer had affected my life; of particular relevance in developing my analytical guides was that it had been her story I turned to in order to draw some contrasting questions when reading Novas and Rose's (2000) paper. My story of my mother's cancer had come together with Novas and Rose's article to provide the genesis of my analytical attitude. However, around a third of the way through the recruitment process I gained a further significant companion story: My Cancer. The story of my mother's cancer became my 'old' story and My Cancer my 'new' story: 'Old stories *take their place* in a past that is still resonant but no longer has the power to set parameters of the future' (Frank, 2010: 158, emphasis in original). So, upon returning to my research this dichotomy between my personal story and my analytical guides evolved once more.

Becoming a wounded ethnographer

As discussed, the question that orientated my reflections soon after my differential diagnosis of testicular cancer was: what difference does this make to me and to my research? Embarking upon an unintended ethnographic study appeared, perversely, to be an exciting opportunity. Following Sontag's metaphor, cancer was a passport to a new world. One, granted, that no one – including myself – wished to go to. But, as I had been bundled aboard and was disembarking, I could not help but reflect that it would provide new forms of stories and an opportunity to explore new modes of analysis (Gale, 2010).

Apart from the opportunity to engage a new research method, there was also the question of what 'difference' this made to my analytical attitude, as well as to my relations to those I interviewed in my research. Of course some things had changed, but even more had stayed the same. What troubled me from my diagnosis onwards was how I could respond to the qualitative researcher's need to 'account' for my unintended analytical companion. But when I reflected upon this I came to realize that it was the way the expectation of difference first presented itself to me as a methodological problem that was, itself, the problem that I now encountered. What these unusual circumstances permitted was not just the acute examination of the position of the researcher turned subject, but of the epistemological soup that constitutes 'doing' qualitative research. In particular, what made Frank's (1995: 2) approach apposite was that he also differentiates how telling a story is 'not just *about* illness. The story was told *through* a wounded body. The stories that ill people tell come out of their bodies. The body sets in motion the need for new stories when its disease disrupts the old stories' (emphasis in original). What appeared to make matters more problematic, however, was the fact that both the storyteller and the listener were similarly wounded bodies.

For myself, my new analytical guide was that I had come to embody my field – I had become a 'wounded ethnographer'. My newly scarred and damaged body allowed me access to new places where stories of CAM and cancer were told. It enabled me to take part and be caught up in some of these stories, to struggle with their multiple ethical demands and to wrestle with how I came to think of myself as forming my subjectivity. But Frank (2010) warns that those who, like himself, were previously familiar with illness due to their research background and who then became ill, should not look to take on the position of expert or authority on similar matters. In my analysis, as in the fieldwork, the attitude I took to my previous experiences and knowledge was that my old stories were only tools – or a toolbox of stories – via which I could put my experiences into words. Neither my companion illness nor my analytical attitude allowed me to substitute the stories of people I met with any of my own. In many ways I considered this to be no different to the attitude I took to my research prior to My Cancer. Yet I suspected that my analytical attitude had changed, as my relationship with the field was different, and because my body had changed.

In the CAM and self-help groups we spent some time exploring what it was to become bodily aware or develop what Frank (1995) calls 'bodily relatedness'. But this was less of a challenge to the story as, after all, My Cancer started with an acute episode of bodily awareness. In the groups such bodily awareness practices, worked on using visualizations and meditations, were related somewhat to 'other-relatedness' (Frank, 1995). Here, the embodied dyadic relations to other persons were explored. Again, this group work did not contest previous stories that worked for me. I was not unfamiliar with experiences of sharing the messy and intimate 'otherness' of people's bodies. However, a final concern of the groups was with the exercises that sought to re-animate the person, to reconnect them with their desires and drives after the flattening effects of cancer treatment upon a person's affect. This work looked to explore the purpose one found for one's life through visualizations and small group discussions. This was a 'compelling' open-ended narrative that sought to invoke from within you a renewed or new purpose to life, which we were told held both transformational and transcendental possibilities.

That is to say, the fieldwork and the interviews were as much a bodily experience as they were about listening to and telling stories. The body was worked upon to both fully hear and express the stories it had to tell, and also to affect it through the stories that were told. What was being produced was not, say, the imposition of a psychoanalytical body (cf. Walkerdine, 2010), but the opening of new ethical possibilities for the body. To paraphrase Frank (1995: 40), a distinct tension was ever present between the expressions of being told how to have cancer, and being shown that you can have cancer in another (better) way – often a way that sought to reaffirm the humanity within and between members of the group.

The problem that My Cancer brought to the fore for the analysis – a problem that is present in most qualitative research, but rarely in such an acute way – is the researcher's own physical investment in the stories they hear. What became apparent in my analytical guides was my sociological desire to hear stories in a certain way, to hear them end in particular ways, or the wish to tell or be told a certain story. Being aware of the normative affectivity in my sociological imagination became a key attitude that I sought to develop.

What was therefore necessary was an emphasis in the field and in the analysis on how embodied, non-discursive affect of stories were experienced. This can start with a discursive exploration of the feelings stories generate, but the distance between my companion illness and analytical guides highlighted the impossibility that is found in a story's ability to actually narrate that embodied affective moment. What needed to be recognized in the analysis were the ways that stories are able to show, but not fully tell, how users of CAM and self-help *feel*. An attitude to analysis that allowed for the productive possibilities that this descriptive failure held was therefore needed.

* * *

It was not possible to provide a formalized method for the analysis I conducted, and not simply because it would be, at best, disingenuous to argue that having the very illness you are researching mid-way through the fieldwork is a valid or reliable process for research. However, this did not stop the product of such reflections from providing a useful analysis, as long as the account that describes how the analysis flowed between the inside and outside can be trusted (cf. Back, 2007). Here I echo Frank (2010) once more in attesting that in such circumstance it is the formation of a particular *attitude* that needs to be conveyed when exploring how the researcher's stories and experiences are part of constituting the analytical account.

The analytical guides I sought to develop aimed to provide a situated account, rather than a revealing look inside a person's head or a debunking of the pseudo-reality of the field. The struggle was to find an attitude that could recognize the interviewee's story as their own, while also recognizing the impact of my companion illness in framing their story and our narratives. How their stories intersected with my analytical attitude was therefore part of forming my analytical guides. The analysis that I developed was recognizably only one understanding; its contingencies open to further interpretation, not only by the interviewee or myself, but also by the reader. What resulted was not a representation of what occurred, it was a reconstituting of the stories I heard into my analytical account. This necessitated that I accepted that these formed new renderings. I had not 'stripped away' things to 'reveal' what was 'actually there'. Rather, my analysis *added* to that field (Latour, 2004); I certainly did not stand neutrally separate from it.

References

Back, L. (2007) *The Art of Listening*. Oxford: Berg.

Frank, A. W. (1991/2002) *At the Will of the Body: Reflections on Illness*. New York: Mariner Books.

Frank, A. W. (1995) *The Wounded Storyteller: Body, Illness and Ethics*. London: The University of Chicago Press.

Frank, A. W. (2010) *Letting Stories Breathe: A Socio-Narratology*. London: Chicago University Press.

Gale, N. K. (2010) 'The Embodied Ethnographer: Journeys in a Health Care Subculture', *International Journal of Qualitative Methods* 9(2): 206–23.

Goffman, E. (1963/1990) *Stigma: Notes on the Management of Spoiled Identity*. London: Penguin.

Harrington, A. (2008) *The Cure Within: A History of Mind Body Medicine*. London: W. W. Norton and Co.

Latour, B. (2004) 'Why Has Critique Run out of Steam? From Matters of Fact to Matters of Concern', *Critical Inquiry* 30(2): 225–48.

LeShan, L. (1994) *Cancer as a Turning Point: A Handbook for People with Cancer*. New York: Plume.

Novas, C. and Rose, N. (2000) 'Genetic Risk and the Birth of the Somatic Individual', *Economy and Society* 29(4): 485–513.

Rabinow, P. and Rose, N. (2003) 'Introduction: Foucault Today', in P. Rabinow and N. Rose (eds) *The Essential Foucault: Selections From The Essential Works Of Foucault, 1954-1984*, pp. vii–xxxv. New York: New York Press.

Sontag, S. (1979/2009) *Illness as Metaphor and AIDS and Its Metaphors*. London: Penguin Classics.

Walkerdine, V. (2010) 'Communal Beingness and Affect: An Exploration of Trauma in an Ex-industrial Community', *Body and Society* 16(1): 91–116.

She and I
Composite Characters in Creative Non-Fiction

Katie Karnehm

On a wet October day in Scotland, a girl opens her second storey window and leans out, smelling all the world's synonyms for wet. Mulch. Grass. Wet leaves piled along what she now knows to call pavement. Wet dog. Wet wool. All the wet people huddled under waterproof jackets and soggy hoodies. She pulls her head back inside the window and pushes it down, but not all the way. Edinburgh is a battle between wet and warm and musty. Sometimes with the windows closed tight the house is just as cold as if they are open. So she keeps a window open and listens to the hiss of tires on wet roads compete with the hum of the radiator.

Back at her writing desk, she puts her pen to her mouth, then hunches over the paper, doodling. The city is loud this morning. The rain amplifies the sounds of cars, horns, tires, shouting pedestrians, even as it hushes them. The longer she is here the more contrasts she finds in her new home.

* * *

The click of the heating reminds me another hour has passed and my 1000-word writing assignment for the day still is not finished. I am writing a story about students who travel to Europe for a semester or year abroad, but I am missing something significant – a lead character, capable of carrying the plot, loose as it is; tethers of real life dangle out of the narrative like a half-knitted scarf. After interviews with dozens of students in nine countries, many interesting stories float to the surface, but none of them is enough to tie the whole narrative together. I'm looking for a character. *Draw a picture of her*, a voice in my head tells me. When I do, I find a character made out of bits: the girls in Amsterdam plus the girl in Scotland combined with another in Italy. Certain details of this character's narrative come from the survey responses of two classes of students in Italy. When I sit down and try to determine which details to include and which to leave out, I seem to hear them all saying, *Tell our stories*. None of them, however, wants to be the star. So I start writing again, focusing on the sound of the rain and not the washing machine in the kitchen below, not the coffee pot switching off, not the mail sliding through the door slot. By noon, one pseudo-imaginary character takes on the characteristics of 20-some people, one of which is me.

The sound of the mail slot, the washing machine, the coffee pot and the rain on the skylight come straight from my own life as a graduate student in Scotland and northern England. So do the scenes from the window. However, the stories of getting pick-pocketed in Rome, getting yelled at by an old lady on the tram, and missing the last train home from the Snoop Dogg concert in Amsterdam come straight from my conversations with students, friends and former classmates who studied abroad. Sometimes they fit best as part of a narrative of one central student who, depending on the reading of the story, has either never existed, or always did. When writing about transcultural experiences, composite characters can help convey common experiences and truths in organized ways, but the specificities of the experiences of many, applied to one, draw attention to the sometimes uncomfortable way that creative non-fiction blurs the distinction between fact and fiction in dynamic, if unpredictable, ways. As an author, what are my responsibilities when it comes to reorganizing others' experiences to create a single narrative?

When I created my composite character, I envisioned a dark-haired girl from somewhere in the Midwest who goes to the UK for a study abroad semester. Like many such students, she is female, studies the liberal arts, and comes from a financially stable (if not rich) family. I made these choices because as an author I could identify with her, and I felt that if I was taking the liberty to create a character in a non-fiction work, it should be a character whose experience I could understand. For the same reason, she is single, quiet but opinionated, and simultaneously loves visiting new places while also being scared of them. Because I wanted to be honest, I knew it was important that this character had weaknesses – she can whine about cultural differences, she can drink too much, she can spend far more time talking to American friends than the locals she lives with, and like most study abroad students, she can complain about how much academic work she has to do during what is supposed to be her fun semester abroad.

When I started writing about the study abroad experience the composite character that I employed felt real to me. Several years later, however, she feels like a gimmick, and I wrestle with what to do with her – cut her out entirely, leave her in entirely, or use her less. What is becoming clear is that if I am going to consider myself part of the story, I have to write myself into it. I once thought the composite character did that but recently I have changed my mind.

When I started writing my book, I wanted to answer a few questions that had been haunting me since I had studied abroad as a college senior in 2001: Why was study abroad so important to me? What did I learn? Why do I feel like I changed so much? To answer those questions, I travelled around Europe interviewing American study abroad students. This process provided extensive breadth of information but not close insight into what study abroad feels like. Because I had been a study abroad student, I wrote my own experiences into the narrative but not as myself. Rather than writing the story of me studying abroad, I wanted to write the story of all of us.

The result, *Not Drowning but Waving*, is two books between two covers: a lyrical creative piece and a narrative journalistic account of study abroad by Americans in Europe. One key story is the facts, trends, statistics and real people who have done this. The other story is of the experience and how, despite the many differences in a student's journey abroad, study abroad sojourns are much more alike than they are different. To show this, each chapter alternates between two different sections: literary journalism sections composed of interviews with students, quotes, descriptions of places and statistics; and a lyrical nonfiction section, describing the experiences and day-to-day activities of an unnamed third-person composite character. This character is composed of students I met and experiences I had. The goal of using a composite character was to show first-hand what study abroad can look and feel like, as well as to emphasize that the experience of studying abroad brings with it some very similar experiences: the feeling of vulnerability when being out of one's culture, the navigation of a new language and cultural mores, the process of eventually confronting one's identity in another culture's mirror, and deciding what to do about it. By using a third-person composite, I wanted to explore the ties between the author, interviewees and readers.

While writing the book, I thought I was writing the story of other students. Since finishing it, however, I've realized I was actually writing a lot about me. The composite character was good for general details: the train systems in the Czech Republic and England; struggles with language across Europe; dealing with pickpockets in any country. But the weakness of using a composite character is just that – its generality. When I switch from third person to first person, the story instantly takes on more life and detail, and my readers notice it right away. I have to wonder if this is because when I am writing about myself, I feel more comfortable ascribing details to the experience of studying abroad. I can write about the feelings of bewilderment and know I am being true to the experience. I could create a character with a name, birth date, and personal details, and thus *invent* a story that advertises itself as nonfiction.

I would not be the first writer to invent characters in nonfiction. *Old Mr. Flood* by Joseph Mitchell, a story about the old men hanging around the Fulton Fish Market in New York City that focuses on the character of Old Mr. Flood, was one of the first pieces of journalism to employ a composite character. Mitchell wrote his essays in 1944 and published them in book form in 1948. When the articles were first published, they read like journalism, so readers were taken aback when the book was released as 'fiction' and Mr. Flood was revealed as never having existed.

The following is a quote from Mitchell's preface to the book:

> These stories of fish-eating, whiskey, death, and rebirth first appeared in *The New Yorker*. Mr. Flood is not one man; combined in him are aspects of several old men who work or hang out in Fulton Fish Market, or who did in the past. I wanted these stories to be truthful rather than factual, but they are solidly based on facts. (Mitchell, 2005)

Until recent scandals in creative nonfiction, Mitchell's 'deception' has been characterized as part of the New Journalism movement that, according to Gay Talese, 'seeks a higher truth' (O'Rourke, 2003) and in doing so, sometimes made use of composite characters and timelines. In 1984 the *Wall Street Journal* reported that Alastair Reid had invented composite characters, dialogue and some scenes in his non-fiction *New Yorker* articles. In 'A Letter from Barcelona', Reid wrote about the experience of Spanish patrons in a bar heckling a televised speech by General Franco. In an article in *The New York Times* Maureen Dowd writes:

> Actually, Mr. Reid said ... the bar had closed by then and he had watched the speech on a friend's television set – the man who had been the bartender. He had created the scene as a composite, distilling things that he had seen and heard in different places. (Dowd, 1984)

Reid's response, in an interview with *Wall Street Journal* reporter Joanne Lipman was, 'You have to get over this hump that it's fact or else ... There is a truth that is harder to get at and harder to get down towards than the truth yielded by fact' (Means, 1984).

On July 28, 2003, Vivian Gornick spoke to a group of students at Goucher College about her use of composite characters, and horrified them when she said that she had used composite characters in her memoir *Fierce Attachments* (Sterling, 2003). She horrified them further when she said she had fudged time, chronological details and certain events for the benefit of the story – and had also used those devices in various journalistic articles for the *Village Voice*. Since then, Augusten Burroughs and several other nonfiction writers have admitted to using composite characters. Burroughs, who '[merged] a couple of ad people together into one', states his reasoning as, 'ad people are all pretty similar, so who cares?' (Sterling, 2003).

After her talk at Goucher, Gornick was described as having confessed to inventions in her writing and was criticized for them. Jack Shafer, from *Slate*, presents one view of such invention: that it is wrong to ever do so in any work calling itself non-fiction.

> All fabricators share a common motive: They want to make their story better than the plain truth, which they think gives them license to blend characters into a composite, pipe in dialogue, and edit events into a more logical narrative. If the truth refuses to collaborate, they conjure up something more compelling. (Shafer, 2003)

Megan O'Rourke, however, defends Mitchell's composite characters and invention by saying that while an emphasis on telling the truth is important, devoting oneself to it at the expense of all else would result in 'an impoverishment of American journalism' (2003). Her take on Mitchell is that 'Mitchell's *Old Mr. Flood* is a world you want to read about not because it's utter fantasy but because it seems real – in fact, it's a world that seems more real, more pressing in its moral accounting than those you find in many well-documented but dull examples of magazine journalism' (O'Rourke, 2003).

Similarly, Gornick defends herself by saying memoir should be evaluated differently from journalism. In several speeches and in an article on Salon.com, she defends her use of composite characters, explaining that real life is the rough draft for a memoir – how you write it matters (Gornick, 2003). Gornick faced a great deal of criticism for her creative choices and her defence of them, and was, in her own words, put in the same category as Jayson Blair, Binjamin Wilkomirski, and Doris Kearns Goodwin, writers who plagiarized or fabricated aspects of their non-fiction pieces in *The New York Times*, a holocaust memoir *Fragments*, and political biographies, respectively (Gornick, 2003). Despite initial surprise from readers that the protagonist of *Old Mr. Flood* was not real, Mitchell's composite work has now been mostly accepted. On the dust jacket of current editions readers are told Old Mr. Flood is a composite, which eliminates any chance of further misunderstandings and also makes the coincidental facts of his life a little easier to accept. Old Mr. Flood has Mitchell's birthday as well as his love for the Bible and Mark Twain, which could be seen as drawing attention to the author's involvement in the manipulation of the character (Shafer, 2003).

My composite character has no name, very few defined characteristics and life details, and fluid life experiences that change with the situation being described in the current chapter, which I feel draws attention to her composition The trouble, of course, is making the idea of her and the people instilled her real enough to care about.

* * *

The girl stands on the edge. Take off. Take flight. Take as little as possible. These instructions chant in her head like falling flowers. She nudges the toe of her Converse in the dirt, and sees how short her tether is. But what she doesn't see is its breaking point. Someday, after she holds her breath and runs as fast and far as possible, she will look back and see the frayed shreds of her leash floating in the waters somewhere behind her.

If she's lucky, someone at the check-in desk will decide she should be in business class. They may not know this is her first flight alone across the Atlantic, or that this seating arrangement is the first of several strokes of good luck she will have during the next harried day. Her plane does not crash. She doesn't lose her luggage, although sometimes she thinks it would be easier if she did. She finds a baggage cart, and only once do her bags tumble off onto the concourse. She gets on the right bus and isn't pick-pocketed on the underground train. Someone agrees to watch her mountain of bags while she hails a cab, and the hostel is actually clean and quiet. The operator puts the call through to her parents, and when she wakes up from a nap in the hostel, another American girl is in the room, ready to make friends.

* * *

I am in the process of writing my experience and myself back into the story. The tricky thing with this story is that I lived the life of a study abroad student (albeit a grown-up one) as I simultaneously interviewed students about theirs. One reason the composite character was tempting was because she could let me move back and forth across the boundary between. So in many ways, my composite character is me ten years ago. When I created her, she was not supposed to be, but the longer I wrote, the more of my personality traits (introversion, independence) and preferences (vegetarianism, ice cream, cathedrals) she took on. The more I have reconciled myself to this fact, the more I have wondered if I should trade the third-person *she* for *I*. However, when writing about a group experience, the choice of a pronoun is not as easy as trading one for the other.

One of the things I was most interested in writing about was my character's first introduction to her new country, and her process of leaving her old country. Almost all of my student interviewees talked about leaving America and arriving in the new country, which was almost always very stressful at first, then amusing later. It seemed that most of the interviewees saw their departure from North America as a key first step in changing while abroad. I wanted my readers, who I mostly saw as former, current and future students, to think *Yes, that's exactly what it felt like* when they read that section, and in some ways I felt like I could better express that via a character.

Another reason I wanted a composite was because during my research I was asked again and again to describe one 'typical' or 'ideal' student I had met during my research. I never could, because he or she does not exist. Despite similar situations and experiences, no two study abroad experiences are identical or can be interpreted the same way. At the time I believed (and to some extent still do, based on my interviews with students) that most extended sojourns abroad contain important similarities. As in the hero's journey archetype, the traveller is called to leave. The traveller encounters adversity such as no wifi and no Thanksgiving break, trivial things that give way to culture shock and homesickness. The traveller encounters successes like learning to speak Italian to the barista, the thrill of discovering new places and making friends from all over the world. Finally she achieves her goal, whatever that may be, which becomes the resolution to the story. In most students' cases, this is the triumphant return to America that turns bittersweet when they discover how much they have changed and how much home has not. The famous hero's journey ends in wisdom, but not always a happy-ever-after conclusion. Study abroad students often say they feel lost in their own countries even while they can culturally adapt anywhere else.

The stories of my character's life and the way they are written reflect the study abroad experience. She portrays common experiences but is not all-knowing; she makes mistakes, does not know how to handle the next challenge and frequently does things she is not proud of, like getting into a spat with a train conductor or her roommate. Because this character is absorbed in the present moment and the differences and challenges and excitements that she is facing, her story happens in present tense. In places where I needed to write about cultural issues specific to a certain place, I imagined her visiting those places, basing her experience on the experiences of others.

Throughout the work, I wanted readers to clearly see she was an invention. I never gave her a name, and very little personal history. In the sections where I used her, I began with phrases like, 'let's imagine for a minute' or 'pretend that'. Statements like these act as signals to the reader to ensure they are aware that this is not a real person but a very real experience. In my opinion, including this kind of clarification might be the only ethical way to use a composite in creative non-fiction.

* * *

She prides herself for moving through crowds without a grope or a wink; she prides herself on going many days without getting hassled. So eventually she gets lazy, dresses like an American girl, carries her camera like a tourist, and pride comes before a fall. The man selling leather jackets propositions her outside his shop; the man at Piazza Michelangelo suggests with a wink that they 'tour' Florence tomorrow. She walks alone in Brussels, clutching the best waffle in the world when a wolf-pack of men walks towards her. The shore of the other side of the street is too far away. All she can do is keep walking, even when one breaks ranks just long enough to run at her shouting in drunken French. She huddles further into her coat and walks faster.

Harassment is a possibility that never seems to be far from her thoughts, even when sleeping. Vigilance borne of constant warnings makes her dream of walking in marketplaces with her sisters, asking directions from a man who keeps trying to yell at her, grab her and finally grope her. 'You idiot,' she finally screams, flashing a plain gold wedding band, 'I have this. I'm married. You're supposed to leave me alone.'

* * *

In my book, the composite character is made up of me, many of the students I interviewed, and some of the students I never met because they responded via an email questionnaire. In the narrative journalism section of each chapter, I often identified these students by their first names because they had given an important quote or had a unique story to tell. In the literary non-fiction section, I amalgamated them into the composite character as best I could without making her too generic or schizophrenic. I found practical reasons for using her too. I could give detailed descriptions about certain study abroad experiences while still protecting student anonymity. It also allowed me to participate in the story without turning the story into a memoir; it was important that the story stayed about the many experiences of studying abroad, not *my* experience of studying abroad.

An issue I experienced was to transpose the most interesting and telling incidents described by students into the narrative of my composite character. I put her in a homestay in France, and try to describe her reaction to others' lived experiences: 'When she takes two pastries at breakfast, Madam raises her eyebrows. When she asks for cream in her coffee in the evening, Madame makes a gusty noise. When she comes home from the supermarket with a tiny jar of peanut butter, exclaiming how unexpectedly small it is, Madam says, "That's because in France, we would never put so much of something so fattening directly in our bodies."' This story is a summary of three people's stories, and I wonder if, in the process, I have focused on experiences to understand rather than characters to care about.

* * *

The main challenge for the young women I have been talking to about France is the French people. 'It's hard because they're not really friendly,' Amanda says. 'In the States we complain that people aren't genuine – but I'm like, "please be un-genuine but just be nice!"'

Amanda and Kristin also don't like 'how women are treated and talked to – it disgusts me. They think we're at their disposal. And my teacher is an avid cigarette smoker.'

'I like the sugar and lemon crepes though,' Kristin said.

'I've liked everything I've eaten here,' Amanda says. 'Especially the *éclairs* at Bernhard's. But not the random hours that stores close.'

Later, long after I have asked my questions and they have processed their answers for me, I go to art class with Amanda where she translates occasionally for me while I take notes in English and wish I had studied abroad at a language school. Afterwards we go to lunch, where to her horror I get the cashier to break a twenty-euro note for me and I buy her lunch. We eat on a bench along the main boulevard and observe the market. She humours me when I want to take photographs of the flowers in the many squares connecting the dots of Aix, and, after bread and cheese sandwiches, we go to Bernhard's for pastries. It's Lent, and I gave up sugar, but I'm also in France. I tell God I'm sorry and cross myself, then buy myself a giant chocolate *éclair*.

* * *

Perhaps the best example of the fusion of characters that make up my composite character comes from the conclusion. In it are stories from my own experience (cycling to a pub in the dark, downhill in the rain, walking around Amsterdam at midnight), stories from the experiences of three boys driving through the countryside not knowing how to reverse the car, and the stories of two girls tracking down the Blarney stone. When I think of the fleeting nature of a semester abroad and the carefree, risk-taking and ultimately adventurous attitude that comes with it, I think of these stories that I either lived or heard. Sometimes, the spirit of my story combines with the details of others, and I become very aware of how my composite character gets to experience both. Maybe this is why at the very end of my story, the pronouns change from 'I' and 'she' to simply 'you'.

* * *

A year before she had never dreamed that she would drive across Ireland, much less drive across Ireland without knowing how to reverse the rental car. She didn't know she would coast downhill in the rain around Loch Lomond, spinning the wheels of her rental bike while the lorries flew past. She didn't foresee cycling to the pub in the dark or walking to Amsterdam at midnight, making her way back to a temporary home one bike light, one night bus, one stranger at a time. She never realized she knew so little about driving a stick shift, or talking to strangers, or taking her life into her hands. But what do you do when 4000 miles out, hell bent on the Blarney Stone and the ring of fire and the graves of the heroic dead? If you can go forward, you go forward. You pull sideways up along the most necessary stopping points, then pull straight out again the next morning, racing toward another crumbled castle on a hill.

References

Dowds, Maureen (1984) 'A Writer For The New Yorker Says He Created Composites In Reports', *NYTimes.com*, accessed July 2013, www.nytimes.com/1984/06/19/nyregion/a-writer-for-the-new-yorker-says-he-created-composites-in-reports.html.

Gornick, Vivian (2003) 'A Memoirist Defends Her Words', Salon.com, accessed July 2013, http://www.salon.com/writer/vivian_gornick/

Means, Howard (1984) 'Truth with a Wink', *The Day*, accessed May 2012, http://news.google.com/newspapers?nid=1915&dat=19840623&id=PjVSAAAAIBAJ&sjid=OzYNAAAAIBAJ&pg=1944,4850015

Mitchell, Joseph (2005) *Old Mr. Flood*. San Francisco, CA: MacAdam/Cage.

O'Rourke, Megan (2003) 'Literary License: Defending Joseph Mitchell's composite characters', *Slate.com*, accessed July 2013, http://www.slate.com/articles/arts/culturebox/2003/07/literary_license.html

Shafer, Jack (2003) 'The Fabulous Fabulists: Mencken, Liebling, and Mitchell made stuff up, too. Why do we excuse them?', *Slate.com,* accessed July 2013, http://www.slate.com/articles/news_and_politics/press_box/2003/06/the_fabulous_fabulists.html

Sterling, Terry Green (2003) 'Confessions of a Memoirist', *Salon.com,* accessed July 2013, http://www.salon.com/writer/terry_greene_sterling/

More Lies Please
Biography and the Duty to Abandon Truth

Rodge Glass

> Truth is mighty and will prevail. There is nothing the matter with this, except that it ain't so. (Mark Twain's notebook, 1898)

I was up early this morning. The kind of early where you find yourself wandering the streets, eyes stinging from tiredness, counting down the minutes in the half-light until the coffee shops open and the city wakes slowly up. I'm not often in the West End of Glasgow these days but last night I stayed with a pal in Partick, so found myself back where I lived as an undergraduate. I delayed heading home to the South Side for the rest of the morning. Instead, I gravitated towards streets I used to walk when I was writing my biography of Alasdair Gray (2005–8), a period which now seems so long ago I sometimes feel sure it was the life of another man.[1] I read the paper, sent a few emails on my phone, and my mind flitted back and forth between various jobs up ahead in the next few weeks – an essay, some book events, the paper on which this is chapter is based. Then I got an idea. I decided to pop into the old Postgraduate room of the Scottish Literature Department in Glasgow University. I'd left something on the shelf four years ago and wondered whether it was still there.

While writing my PhD (a more academic version of the Gray biography titled *Working With Alasdair Gray*),[2] I spent many hours working in that room, with several dedicated others who were also writing projects about Scottish authors (Hugh MacDiarmid, Iain Banks, William Soutar), each project with an element of biography to it. I also used the space at nights to write my second novel *Hope for Newborns*, so probably spent more time there than was healthy, but most times I had company, and these other students influenced my own writing, partly because being in that building with them made it impossible to escape a sense of duty. The Scottish Literature library was above us – Welsh, Burns, Kelman lived up there, along with Galloway, Spark and Kennedy. Liz Lochhead had a spell as Writer-in-Residence in the building. Meanwhile, the other offices were occupied by academics who'd made a life's work of trying to get at the meaning behind the work of great literary Scots. As we were often reminded, this was the only Scottish Literature Department in the world. Which also brought responsibilities. If that sounds self-important, it's not meant to – our little room had half a dozen old computers, one kettle, three shelves, a musty smell, a window that only half-opened, and a few ripped posters on the walls. We were usually low on coffee. None of us had much money or serious ambition to make any. But the atmosphere was warm, and we chatted often about the challenges of each project, sometimes discussing what might have happened in the life of one writer or another for hours at a time. We talked about the dead ones as if they were alive and the live ones as if they were in the room with us. We felt a sense of responsibility, as Hilary Mantel put in her memoir *Giving Up the Ghost* – and as quoted by Helen Pleasance elsewhere in this book – 'to get it right' (Mantel, 2003: 5). But this sense of responsibility has little to do with the word 'truth' and that this is nothing to feel uncomfortable about.

The 'Determining Form' conference was one of the few times I had been back to the Glasgow University campus since completing my project there. I remember wondering, while giving the address, whether my original manuscript was still in the old office – I'd left the only copy there in 2008 and had been meaning to get it – but thought surely it would have been binned or lost since. Besides, in the past I'd told myself that this 'original' version was not so original anyway. It was simply one saved file among hundreds that I just so happened to have printed off and bound. This version from 22/11/07 was never published, no one had read the whole thing apart from me,[3] and the book had been rewritten and edited many times after that – by me, with additional suggestions made by my supervisors and also my editor at Bloomsbury.[4],[5] So why search it out at all? Well, this morning, in my sleepy, cloudy mood, it occurred to me that investigating this previous incarnation of what I had since come to think of as a fixed, unmoving thing would be a good way to examine how writing biography complicates ideas of truthfulness and historical accuracy. After all, if I had written several different versions of scenes in which AG and I were characters, containing different descriptions of our movements, statements and actions, implying different subtext and meaning, which one of these could be called 'true'? A recorded transcript containing the literal truth, a written draft that strived to get close to the truth, or a final edit which abandoned that search altogether? All of these? One of them? None? A friendly cleaner with a master key let me into the Postgrad room on the sly (I'd forgotten the code for the door) and I saw that, though things had changed a little, they hadn't changed that much – and my manuscript was exactly where I'd left it.

When I picked up that early version of the biography, the first thing I noticed was its weight. At 140,000 words it was 40,000 fatter than what I submitted to Bloomsbury, and at least 20,000 longer than the version I submitted for my PhD. For starters, I'd included many lengthy diary entries that later had to be deleted – that version was full of melodrama, overstatement, self-doubt, and it focused too much on how I felt about the minutiae of Gray's daily existence, which, with a few years' distance, I can now see didn't add to an understanding of the man – they were only relevant to how I personally coped with the process of writing about him. My worries about Alasdair's minor health problems, read years after he recovered from them, would not be interesting to the vast majority of people. Especially given that there was already a full chapter in the final published version entitled 'Health'. But rereading this material, I realized that not only did Gray's life contain many possible as-yet-unwritten biographies, but I had also begun, then abandoned, so many of them that I had simply wiped most of these from my mind – until now. Perhaps this is understandable: no author can contain entire books in their head at any one time, never mind multiple discarded drafts. But still, the Alasdair Gray I had been presenting to people at readings, book festivals and in interviews since 2008 was not a coherent person at all. He was many people, each a slightly different mix of the man, my imagination and my ability (or lack of it) to articulate that on the page. The AG of the inside page poem entry (Glass, 2008), the AG of the mock play script diary entry (Glass, 2008: 30-1) and the AG of the final diary entry (Glass, 2008: 312-3) were each a different kind of real.

All of which is fine. Because a good biography has a number of responsibilities: first, to the subject, second, to the author, and third, to what I call a kind of spiritual truth. But a good, honest biography also has a fourth, crucial responsibility that many writers forget: to be readable. Something my book would not have been had it included several chapters of late-night tortured anguish about the nature of my relationship with Alasdair, self-obsessed doubt over whether I was capable of finishing the project, or pages of hand-wringing over whether I had got an important date wrong. It also would have been worse off for including several near-identical chapters about Gray's public appearances where, I noticed after a while, he would often repeat the same answers, almost word for word, regardless of the question.[6] It may seem blindingly obvious to state, but a biography is, at its most basic level, a book – not a life at all. It's a series of sometimes-disputed fragments greatly condensed, shaped, magicked from experience into words, not a photograph or a mirror of an entire existence. There is no such thing, and anyone who tells you differently is the real liar in this ongoing debate about 'truth'.

In a way, it's similar to the debate going on in contemporary fiction about the duty of the writer to represent historical events 'truthfully', a debate given more urgency by the case of the novelist David Peace. Peace was successfully sued by the ex-Leeds United player John Giles for how he is portrayed in scenes from Peace's novel *The Damned United,* which was later made into a film directed by Tom Hooper and starring Michael Sheen. The explanation 'this is a fiction based upon a fact',[7] which Peace always includes at the back of his books, was enough for fiction audiences, but was not acceptable to judges of both book and film who wanted to know for sure whether what they were reading about or seeing was really 'true'. It was also not acceptable to a furious Giles, who said he had been portrayed as a 'scheming leprechaun'. In an interview with the *Independent* to promote his book *A Football Man: The Autobiography*, Giles explained how Peace's novel and the successful legal case that followed had prompted him to reply with his side of the story:

> Peace said the novel was fiction based upon fact. Trouble is, people assume it's the official version. The movie was a misinterpretation of the misinterpretation that was the book! ... It never happened. It was ridiculous. (Shaw, 2010)

This high-profile case was controversial, and it made the new Legal Department at Bloomsbury even more risk-averse than usual when going through the possible legal implications of my own book – fictionalizing the lives of the long dead was a profitable, mostly safe business, but dealing with the lives of the living was something else entirely. The case may also appear to have knock-on effects for more traditional biographical forms, and cases such as that of David Peace certainly made things spicier for me, but I'd argue that – though it's important to be clear with readers about the bargain being entered into when they open up a book of any kind – biographers should resist pressures to define the real and the unreal in terms John Giles would find acceptable. Far better to embrace uncertainty when it rears its head. Far better to seek out those in-between spaces and look for wider truths, rejecting simplistic, narrow definitions which assume that one individual's truth is the same as the man standing next to him.

The responsibility of the modern biographer is not to stand on the top of the mountain and deliver the gospel, it's to capture the flavour of the subject and their work – to draw out meaning from events, documents, interviews and anything else that can be made use of. I chose to do this in a way that I hoped Gray fans would recognize and enjoy, imitating my subject's language, tone and preferred fictional structures in how I put the book together. I saw my responsibility to myself as exactly the same thing as my responsibility to readers: to entertain, and to convey the spirit of Alasdair Gray the man for those who might never have the opportunity to meet him, while making a thorough, unapologetic, critical analysis of his literary works, something which had not been attempted before. Hence the structure of half a traditional academic biography, half a themed diary. Hence the focus on watching him paint, driving him to a friend's funeral, reviewing his public performances, interviewing him about his mother over a dram of whisky. Hence using his poem '1st March 1990' (Gray, 2000: 1) to analyse his exhaustion with writing at a key point in his career.[8] Hence using a little-known 1986 rant in an exhibition pamphlet to analyse whether Gray rated his Art School crowd too highly (Glass, 2009: 82). Every one of the sections named here would not have made the cut in a biography that claimed to deal in 'absolute truth'. Which is exactly why I'm interested in them.

But there's a big difference between beautiful lies and simply lying. So it's important to be able to distinguish between the two.

Rereading that old version of my biography this morning, I noticed something I'd totally forgotten I'd done. In early versions of many diary entries I'd trimmed some of Alasdair's words within quotation marks, to make them read more smoothly – and while noticing this I turned cold and looked around, as if expecting to see another, better scholar standing behind me, head shaking solemnly and muttering, *Oh no, you didn't do THAT did you?* Had I done something terribly wrong? Was this a betrayal of truthfulness, or just a practical, ordinary part of the writing process, part of the responsibility to be succinct? Suddenly, I wasn't sure. Anyone who has ever conducted a conversation with Alasdair, seen him do a reading, watched a documentary about him or heard him speak on the radio will notice he is unusually difficult to edit into digestible chunks. He will often digress, remain silent for several seconds at a time, repeat himself, or simply not answer the question at all. (One interview with Mark Lawson in 2007 for Radio 4's Front Row was pulled entirely because Alasdair could not be persuaded to answer questions directly.)[9] If I'd rendered his speech exactly as it sounded on these pages, then published them, replete with every stutter and delay, then the entire book would have looked like I was mocking him – which I had no desire to do.

Back in 2007, the drafting process became more intense as I got closer to deadline, and I remember increasingly going out of my way to avoid making Alasdair seem like the kind of eccentric cartoon he was sometimes portrayed as in the press. Instead, I tried to find meaningful ways of investigating his mannerisms, making sense of them, trying to decode them. For example, I used his responses to questions asked during a 2007 Glasgow Book Festival event and intercut these with quotations from his Saltire Society Self Portrait in order to illustrate his high level of self-awareness, and how he often used verbal tics in order to get away with things he really believed – by making them appear like jokes (Gray, 1988).[10]

As for the actual selection of words used, I opted for an approach influenced by James Kelman's rendering of language in his novels. Instead of writing every word in the accent he intends his readers to read in, Kelman selects individual Scots words, often specifically Glaswegian words, used in key places, in among what might be termed 'standard English'. The prominent Kelman critic Simon Kovesi has noted how Kelman avoids intrusive rendition, choosing not to transcribe his characters' language phonetically because that would distract from the art in his text. In his book *Contemporary British Novelists: James Kelman* he explains the approach thus:

> Kelman's fictional texts are not voiced in standard English, or in standard Scots: occasionally pockmarked by quasi-phonetic rendition, and linguistic markers of locality – always of Glasgow where recognisable – the voices are broadly variable, polyvalent, inconsistent, and rendered in fluid, changing Kelmanese, a style all of his own making. There is nothing 'pure' about his language other than its consistent idiosyncrasy. (Kovesi, 2007: 21)

I'm fond of this description, and I realize now that I wanted to replicate Kelman's idiosyncratic, 'pockmarked' approach in a biographical context, inventing a sort of Gray-ese along the way. So when laying out Alasdair's speech on the page, I chose to occasionally leave in the odd stutter, repeat or Grayism to portray the tone of his speech, rather than interpret truth literally – which would have included many more interruptions, instantly making my text and all my interviews with Alasdair unreadable. I did this because I felt my responsibility to 'truth', in the context of a 400-page book about a man with a stutter, could only lead me to a hybridized approach, seeking a kind of authenticity by blending the 'real' with the spirit of what I interpreted to be AG's meaning. This is an issue investigated by Bryony Stocker (2012) in her forthcoming essay 'Bygonese', which deals with dialogue and authenticity. Stocker writes specifically about historical fiction, but similar challenges apply equally to Hilary Mantel and to David Peace as they do to the contemporary biographer who is more interested in the nature of their subject than in dry facts.

The question of how to portray Gray's language was just one of many issues concerning historical accuracy and responsibility raised during this process. Another key one was the matter of how to portray Alasdair's family. This led to some difficulty – in fact, the only difficulty, as Gray stuck to his promise of not influencing the book before publication or suing me for its contents afterwards. My dilemma was how to portray Alasdair's living family members – indeed, whether to portray them at all. The decision regarding Alasdair's parents and first wife Inge Sorenson were a different, easier matter to decide upon. This was because Alasdair had explicitly referred to them, repeatedly, in his fiction and non-fiction work, and in many interviews over several decades. Both his mother, Amy Gray (neé Fleming), and Inge had entire sections of his debut poetry volume *Old Negatives* named after them. The shadow of Inge dominated his novella *Mavis Belfrage,* as well as many of his plays from the 1970s. She is a continual presence. Alasdair's parents are central characters in Books One and Two of his career-defining novel *Lanark.* So where Alasdair had already included them in his literary story, as it were, I felt these were fair game.

Questions about Andrew, Alasdair's only child, and Morag, his second wife, were more complicated, mainly because they hardly feature in his work. Aside from the poem 'To Andrew, Before One', also from *Old Negatives,* and some short scenes in *Lanark* and *Mavis Belfrage* that are ambiguous in meaning at best, there is little material either in the work or in biographical interviews which details Alasdair's relationship with his son, who is now grown up and lives in the USA. I didn't feel I could leave him out of the story entirely, especially as he had some valuable insights into what Alasdair was like as a younger man; also because fatherhood changes people, and because Alasdair was very short of money while Andrew was a boy. All of which affected the decisions he made, the commissions he took on, and the way he chose to live after he and Inge got divorced in 1970. But Alasdair had been keener for Andrew to speak to me than Andrew was, and I knew Andrew wasn't entirely comfortable with the existence of my project.[11] This got me thinking about who should be included and why: what kind of book was this after all? What kind of biography? I decided to only include personal details when they illustrated something important about the man or his work that could not otherwise be learned. There was so much to say anyway, and each personal anecdote I included altered the balance of the book. So at the time it felt convenient that Morag had always preferred to keep a low profile, and Andrew the same. It did mean leaving out some details, but then my book was already much too big (Bloomsbury originally set a limit of 100,000 words to save on printing costs), and I didn't feel I had missed anything major that needed to be in the public domain. I interviewed Andrew and Morag, quoted from them both, and that was more than enough. There may come a time when I am interested in saying more, but I suspect that time is a long way off. The crucial thing is that Alasdair has chosen to put himself in the public domain. Neither Morag nor Andrew has, and that is to be respected.

When I completed the final draft of my Gray biography, there were things I could or would not see. For example, I had written the book while Gray was writing, then editing, then publishing and touring his last novel *Old Men in Love*, and I was too close to it to see some weaknesses – even to notice that the reception to it was not as positive as I first imagined. I didn't want to acknowledge negative reviews because it suited the narrative arc of my book to have a kind of a happy ending – I wanted to show my subject going on and on, and still being relevant despite age and claiming to be in decline. That's the one thing I would go back and change if I had the opportunity. As it happened, a happier 'ending' was on its way – just not to my publication schedule.

Since my book was first published, much has changed, and there is now a far more compelling neat narrative to be told about the grand auld boy of Scottish letters. The value of his artwork has shot upwards thanks to the organization and determination of his art agent, Sorcha Dallas, who has set up The Alasdair Gray Foundation and who secured AG his by-far highest profile exhibitions, including being part of The Frieze Art Fair in London in 2008, L'aur'amara in New York in 2010 and The British Art Show in 2011. Meanwhile, his Oran Mor auditorium has become his most popular mural – it was recently filmed for BBC1's The One Show for a package including an interview with AG in April 2011, (2012) something which, in one fell swoop, reached more people in one night than his art has done in the last fifty years. What else? His remarkable autopictography, *A Life in Pictures,* was awarded the Saltire Book of the Year in 2011, though Gray rejected the prize.[11] AG admitted he had started this book as no one else had commented on his art, something which has undoubtedly changed since. So if I'd been finishing my biography now, I would have had a different version again – with a more satisfying end, perhaps. But because I didn't have one in 2008, I sought to create one, weakening the book.

Half of every story is imagined by the listener: I heard what I wanted to hear at that time. In terms of interpreting Alasdair's unusual but intense relationship with his first wife, I should admit that I had clear ideas about love, and what it should be like. I would certainly have written a different book given how my own life has changed since. It may seem like a kind of arrogance to focus so much on my own life in this piece, my own obsessions and experiences when I am supposed to be reflecting on writing someone else's life. Who cares about me? Good question. Well, perhaps no one. But until someone comes up with a way of an omnipotent, neutral super-computer writing biographies, all we have is the human experience, and to pretend that experience is not flawed, and biased, and complicated, and partly in the imagination, is to tell a truly horrible lie.

Leonard Cohen said in a recent interview with the *Guardian,* 'All I have to put into a song is my own experience' (Lynskey, 2012). I'm interested in this statement because it doesn't imply a choice on Cohen's part. He portrays himself as being part of a process he cannot control, and appears to have no desire to. Replace the word 'song' with 'biography' and you have my approach. I believe an author of a biography cannot dispense with any of the authorial choices inherent to other forms of storytelling: you can pretend if you like, you can claim to have all the facts, to sit in the clouds with God and deliver truths from on high, to remain uninfluenced by your background and personal interests and desires, but these statements of undisputed knowledge will be disingenuous. In any biography, which by its very nature must condense and shape a life into tasty chunks, the biographer still chooses what to include, what to omit, how to introduce material and how to order the sequence of events, and can be called upon to justify these choices.

The fields of biography, autobiography, memoir and fiction are ever-shifting, amorphous, and they're mixing up with each other whether the purists like it or not. Some leaders in the field include Darin Strauss, whose searing memoir *Half a Life,* the first line of which is 'Half my life ago, I killed a girl' (Strauss, 2011: 1), pushed the limits of the autobiographical form. An earlier example is Hanif Kureishi's biography of his father, *My Ear at His Heart*. This was Kureishi's truth, but was disputed by other members of his family. Jonathan Coe's biography of B. S. Johnson begins with a young Coe watching Johnson on the television, encouraging readers to see Johnson as the author saw him. And in 2009, David Vann's explosive, genre-busting *Legend of A Suicide* told and retold the suicide of the author's father within the context of a fictional novel, leading Tom Bissell in the *New York Times,* and Angus Linklater in the *Guardian,* to applaud the breaking down of barriers between biographical forms and fiction. I believe these books demonstrate that in order to remain relevant in the twenty-first century, biographical forms need to abandon the high horse approach of previous generations and stop pretending to know everything. It's not big, it's not clever, and it's not real. After all, facts aren't fascinating. People are. Or, as the artist David Hockney put it in a recent interview, 'The most interesting space isn't way out there. It's where I end and you begin' (BBC, 2012). The duty of the contemporary biographer is to climb into that space, see what's there and describe it.

So, I know what I want from biography: more lies please. I want you to lie to me by omission, by inclusion, by the selection of that extra word or phrase that might or might not have been said. Lie to me with a truthful, compassionate heart. Lie to me in order to show me meaning. Why is this okay? Because there is no absolute truth. There's nothing even close to it. I discovered during my extensive interview process for my Gray biography that there are only multiple, conflicting versions of events, usually each one so far from any kind of neutrality that they can hardly be described as truth at all. Let's call biography what it is: a collection of beautiful lies. And let's be at ease with that, because, when done with love and attention to detail, these lies can also have a beautiful shape. And as Picasso reminds us, art is the lie that reveals the greater truth. When you consider his paintings of Dora Maar or Marie Therese Walter it's easy to understand why beautiful lies were essential for Picasso. And they're essential for me too.

As I finally wandered home this morning, the old retrieved Gray manuscript under my arm, my mind began to wander again. And something made me think of those paintings. I remembered seeing a Picasso exhibition in Brisbane last year. In front of one portrait, I stood next to a child who was saying to his father, 'But that's not what a woman looks like!' After a long pause his dad said, 'Well, yes. And no. And yes.' When the father tilted his head, looking back at the painting with a smile, his son copied the movement.

Notes

1 With the exception of a single diary entry from 2004, the biography was written between February 2005 and April 2008, with an update on the biography, 'A Life of Loose Ends' published in Volume 4 Issue 3 of the Scottish Review of Books in 2008 and a Coda written for the paperback in Spring 2009.

2 This included an appendix, references to Gray's never before seen diaries in the National Library of Scotland, and more extensive footnotes considered too detailed for the Bloomsbury version. Unlike most PhDs undertaken there, no copy of this version exists in the Glasgow University library. Before the Bloomsbury version was published in 2008, Univer-

sity administrators were nervous about being sued over the nature of the content.

3 This was not a version for official assessment. I read it, crossed out words, phrases, sections and chapters, then implemented the changes and moved on. This version was printed off because it represented the book at its largest. Though diary entries were written after this date, the master document was much smaller.

4 My supervisors were Professor Willy Maley and Dr Gerard Carruthers.

5 This was Bill Swainson, Chief Commissioning Editor at Bloomsbury Publishing.

6 For the final chapter of the book, 'Not Dead Yet! A Happy Ending, Of Sorts', I followed AG on his tour to promote his new novel *Old Men in Love* (Bloomsbury, 2007).

7 This phrase has been used at the back of a number of David Peace novels, each of which uses historical events as the starting point.

8 '1st March 1990' was later revised in 2005 as part of a series of poems titled 'Selfish Last Verses'.

9 This was part of a 2007 trip to London to promote the publication of *Old Men in Love*.

10 The primary example of this, as detailed in the Saltire Self Portrait, is AG's use of mock accents – Irish, Yankee, posh English, etc. – which he admits he employs as diversionary tactics.

11 This was confirmed when Andrew wrote to the Times Literary Supplement to complain about my book upon publication. Actually, he didn't mind my references to him; he felt protective of his mother, Inge, and felt I had been unfair in my portrayal of her.

12 Gray has been turning down literary prizes (and occasionally accepting them) since the 1980s, claiming he has won enough. In 2011, the board of the Saltire Society politely refused Alasdair's refusal. Once promised he would not have to give a speech, turn up to a prize-giving or have his photo taken (also, after Morag reminded him they could really rather do with £10,000), AG then accepted the award. Though he hoped this could be done quietly, his picture made the front cover of following day's *Times* newspaper in Scotland.

References

Campbell, Alastair (2007) *The Blair Years: Extracts from The Alastair Campbell Diaries*. London: Hutchinson.
Coe, Jonathan. (2004) *Like a Fiery Elephant*, London: Picador.
Lynskey, Dorian. (2012) 'Leonard Cohen: 'All I've got to put in a song is my own experience', *Guardian* (19 January), accessed 12 August 2013, http://www.theguardian.com/music/2012/jan/19/leonard-cohen
Giles, John and Lynch, Declan (2010) *A Football Man: The Autobiography*. London: Hodder & Stoughton.
Glass, Rodge (2008) *A Secretary's Biography*. London: Bloomsbury.
Gray, Alasdair (1981) *Lanark: A Life in Four Books*. Edinburgh: Canongate.
Gray, Alasdair (1986) *Mavis Belfrage: A Romantic Novel with Five Shorter Tales*. London: Bloomsbury.
Gray, Alasdair (1988) *Alasdair Gray (Saltire Pamphlets: Self-portrait Series)*. Glasgow: Morag McAlpine.
Gray, Alasdair (1989) *Old Negatives*. London: Jonathan Cape.
Gray, Alasdair (2000) *Sixteen Occasional Poems*. Glasgow: Morag McAlpine.
Gray, Alasdair (2007) *Old Men in Love*. London: Bloomsbury.
Gray, Alasdair (2011) *A Life in Pictures*. Edinburgh: Canongate.
BBC (2012) *The One* Show (9 May) [Television].
BBC (2012) 'David Hockney: The Art of Seeing – A Culture Show Special', *The Culture Show* (19 April) [Television].
Kovesi, Simon (2007) *Contemporary British Novelists: James Kelman*. Manchester: Manchester University Press.
Kureishi, Hanif (2004) *My Ear at his Heart*. London: Faber.
Mantel, Hilary (2003) *Giving Up the Ghost*. London: Harper Perennial.
Peace, David (2004) *GB84*. London: Faber.
Peace, David (2006) *The Damned United*. London: Faber.
Roth, Philip (1989) *The Facts: A Novelist's Autobiography*. London: Jonathan Cape.
Shaw, Phil (2010) 'Publish and be Damned: Giles fights for Revie and Clough', *Independent*, (13 November), accessed 12 August, http://www.independent.co.uk/sport/football/news-and-comment/publish-and-be-damned-giles-fights-back-for-revie-and-clough-2132719.html
Strauss, Darin (2011) *Half a Life*. London: Beautiful Books Limited.
Stocker, Bryony D. (2012) '"Bygonese" – Is This Really the Authentic Language of Historical Fiction?', *New Writing: The International Journal for the Practice and Theory of Creative Writing*, accessed 12 August 2013,

http://www.tandfonline.com/doi/abs/10.1080/14790726.2012.693094?journalCode=rmnw20#.UgitSayYcx5
Tomalin, Claire (2002) *Samuel Pepys: The Unequalled Self.* London: Viking.
Vann, David (2009) *Legend of a Suicide.* London: Penguin.

Ghosts of the Real
The Spectral Memoir

Helen Pleasance

Hilary Mantel's memoir, *Giving up the Ghost*, begins by expressing the impossible contradiction of the life text. It opens with a self-reflexive meditation on the particular formal and ethical issues for the author of auto/biography. The central issue for such texts is the need to establish a reliable relationship with the reality they purport to represent; as Mantel terms it, 'I need to get it right' (Mantel, 2003/2004: 5). Unlike fiction, the genre in which she usually writes and in which it is accepted that the author makes things up, in memoir there is a particular contractual pressure to give a true account of what really happened in her life. The life genre is dependent upon establishing a reliable relationship between the 'inside' of the text and its 'outside': the real events to which it refers and purports to represent truthfully.[1] Mantel, though, foregrounds the fundamental contradiction of this relationship. The ethical imperative 'to get it right' and tell the truth about one's life is continually thwarted by the form of writing itself. 'Any style you pick seems to unpick itself before a paragraph is done' (Mantel, 2003/2004: 4). In particular she highlights the impossibility of realism as simple mimesis within the life text. For Mantel language always constructs as much as it records, and that is a problem, because it means that what is recorded can never be simply what really happened, and to suggest that it is presents a lie about the past.

The question then becomes how to establish a relationship between the past as it is understood to have happened and as it can be recorded in language. It is as a way of negotiating this relationship that Mantel uses the idea of the ghost. Ghosts haunt her text in various complex ways from the title onwards. But, beyond the appearances of specific ghosts, the book's title, *Giving up the Ghost,* offers a figure for the relationship between language and the past it is attempting to conjure: Mantel cannot pretend that her text is giving readers the past itself, all she can ethically offer is its spectral trace, conjured in the ghost of language.

It is the turn to the motif of haunting in Mantel's and several other recent memoirs (Morley, 2000; Morrison, 1993–2006, 1997) that is addressed here, in order to demonstrate how it has been used to counter the strategies of realism, which seem to present the past as it really was and, thereby, obscure the processes involved in turning experience into textual presence. In presenting the past as spectral these texts lay bare the relationship between text and referent, and suggest that the past is a matter of ontological uncertainty rather than documentary fact. The approach provides a strategy for challenging the certainties of history; in refusing to conjure the past as entirely knowable or as an entity that can be brought to textual presence, these spectral memoirs articulate the losses and disappearances of the past. They present a kind of archive of the lost past, which suggests that there is always something missing from any account of the past. What all these memoirs highlight is the problematic ethics of textual presence in life writing. In rendering events and people in realistic clarity and detail, life writers are using particular fictional strategies. But the fictional strategies of realism can be argued to be invisible; the complex constructions of realism can be easily interpreted as an unproblematic representation of reality as a stable entity external to the text. It is in its invisibility that the power of realism as a representational strategy could be said to lie. Realist texts are inevitably imposing narrative form and structure but they *appear* to summon the real in the text, as if it can be experienced directly. John Tagg, for example, has argued that the power of realism as a representational strategy is in its invisibility:

> It works by the controlled and limited recall of a reservoir of similar 'texts', by a constant repetition, a constant cross-echoing. By such 'silent quotation', a relation is established between the realist 'text' and other 'texts' from which it differs and to which it defers. It is this mutuality which summons up the power of the real.' (Tagg, 1988: 100)

Realism, it could then be argued, is both a way of establishing the reliability of an auto/biographical text (it 'summons up the power of the real') and also rupturing it, if 'the power of the real' is revealed to be a textual strategy.

I, Rigoberta Menchú: An Indian Woman in Guatemala (1984–94) exemplifies the problematic nature of confusing realism with 'the real'. This was a powerful autobiographical account of state atrocities in Guatemala, including Menchú's witness testimony to her brother's murder. Its very title, which repeats the name of the author, seems to summon 'the real' directly and unproblematically. The name refers to both a real person and a textual narrator: 'simultaneously a socially responsible real person, and the producer of a discourse' (Lejeune, 1982: 200). Thus there is a suggestion of a straightforward equivalence between the living Menchú, outside the text, and the Menchú inside the text. *I, Rigoberta Menchú* became a powerful discursive intervention into very real questions of human rights, highlighting, particularly to US readers, the oppression of ethnic groups in Guatemala, allowing them 'an emotional identification with a distant other' (Lauritzen, 2004: 24). The book became a huge historic event, going into more than fifteen reprints in the ten years after its first publication. Menchú went on to win the Nobel Peace Prize in 1992. Elisabeth Burgos-Debray's introduction positions Menchú's story as 'exemplary' of the wider history and politics of indigenous Indians, not just in Guatemala, but 'all the Indians of the American continent' (Menchú, 1984–94: xi). It attests to the text as direct testimony of real events – 'what she has to say is simple and true' (Menchú, 1984–94: xiii) – and establishes the contract of reliable truth telling between author and reader.

However, doubt was cast on the literal truth of all the events narrated in the book, including whether Menchú had actually witnessed her brother's murder. So the strategy by which it gained its political efficacy was also the one that threatened it. Menchú was defended with arguments that this literal reading did not allow for the complex textual strategies at work, in which the narrating I is being used to embody a collective reality of many Guatemalans and to 'testify to a larger truth' (Lauritzen, 2004: 30), which is verifiable. The first-person account, it was argued, was a legitimate fictional strategy, which provided international readers with a powerful textual identification that allowed them an imaginative understanding of real events in Guatemala, and was part of the longer tradition of 'testimonio' writings in Latin America.[2] Significantly, though, this defence had to distinguish between realism as a complex and sophisticated textual negotiation of reality and the book's initial claim that realism could be equated with the 'simple and true' presentation of reality outside the text.

The book's initial claim, to be a direct presentation of real events and people as they really were, and the outcry against the book when that claim was discredited, both indicate a deep desire for the textual possibility that life writing seems to offer. Authors and readers both want it to be possible for texts to recreate exactly that which really happened and once really existed. Jacques Derrida has discussed this as a desire to return to a lost origin; a moment of being that retains significance through remembrance. For Derrida this apparent textual possibility is a myth, because remembrance itself, whether it is as personal memory or as material archive, is a form of entextualization: 'The possibility of the archiving trace, this simple *possibility*, can only divide the uniqueness' (Derrida, 1996: 100). For Derrida it is impossible to make a clear-cut division between referent and text: 'Is there *there*, between the thing itself and its simulacrum, an opposition that holds up?' (Derrida, 1994: 10). The impossibility of making this division leads Derrida to the concept of spectrality; the real haunts all simulacra. Here I will use the trope of 'the thing itself' to express this haunting textual relationship. 'The thing itself' has to be in quotation marks, not just because it is a quote from Derrida, but also because it is always a textual trope, never the thing itself, to which it refers and which is always elusively beyond the text. It expresses the impossibility of representation, and the fantasy of being able to present lived experience textually.

It is for this reason that I turn to what I have termed spectral memoirs, which use different strategies; strategies that open up the space between the text and 'the thing itself', that which is being archived, in order to provide an experience of what happens in that process of archiving. In doing this, these texts might sacrifice the experience of textual presence, but they replace it with an uncanny or spectral experience of reading and its referential relationship to that which is being written about. These texts acknowledge that textual presence can only ever provide a mythical representation of 'the thing itself': the experience, event or person to which the representation refers. They do so through the representation of the complex relationship between the text and its outside as a form of haunting. It is this that gives them claim to an ethical form of truth telling. They engage with past experience as something that shapes the present, and suggest a conceptual framework through which to understand this textual engagement. Louis A. Renza has described autobiography as 'a unique, self-defining mode of self-referential expression, one that allows, then inhibits, its ostensible project of self-representation, of converting oneself into the present promised by language' (Renza, 1980: 295). Here it is useful to expand this definition to life writing more generally. The play between language's promise to convert past reality into textual presence and the inhibition of this promise articulates both the desire to understand the past and the limits that are on this understanding. Every textual engagement with the past represents a particular haunting of it by language. It is by conjuring ghosts that we might articulate our present concerns with past experience.

What prompted Mantel's discussion of her linguistic anxiety caused by life writing was her initial starting point for the text; seeing a ghost of her stepfather. This event is depicted as something that really happened to Mantel; a real experience of haunting. But it is also depicted as something that has a dubious status as verifiable reality, 'I know it is my stepfather's ghost coming down. Or, to put it in a way acceptable to most people, I "know" it is my stepfather's ghost' (Mantel, 2003/2004: 1). Mantel gives a possible rational explanation of the ghost as a hallucination caused by the onset of migraine. But she maintains the ghost as a textual presence, and indeed puts it at the centre of her desire for auto/biographical truth, 'So now I come to write a memoir I argue with myself over every word. Is my writing clear; or is it deceptively clear? I tell myself, just say how you came to sell a house with a ghost in it' (Mantel, 2003/2004: 5). This figure absolutely destabilizes ontology; the 'ghost' has a dubious, possibly only linguistic existence in the realm of real experience (what others might call a visual disturbance, with a neurological explanation, Mantel calls a ghost) but it is this ghost that is brought to textual presence and acts as the figure for the haunted space between the text and its referent. In defining the memoirial project as the desire to write clearly about a haunted house Mantel opens up the textual experience of life writing as uncanny. It is the text itself that is the haunted house, and language the spectral trace of the past that inhabits it.

Mantel uses the uncanny to maintain her text in a state of undecidability. Tzvetan Todorov has discussed the fictional genre of the fantastic as opening up this space of undecidability. Fantastic narratives keep their readers in a state of suspense or uncertainty about mysterious events rendered in the story. Todorov argues that such narratives will either be resolved when a rational explanation is given for the events or when they are explained as supernatural (Brooke-Rose, 1981: 63). Mantel could be said to invoke the fantastic with her introduction of ghosts into the text. But she refuses to give either a rational or a supernatural explanation for them. Her ghosts are maintained as an undecidable presence in the text. Their status is only certain in language, as language. They clearly refer to her dead relatives, but they are neither a supernatural presence nor a neurological symptom; they are a linguistic figure that Mantel uses to render the space between her experience and her memoirial rendition of it.

This provides a powerful strategy for expressing the process of memory (and its failings) and particularly for rendering other people and the past in ways that acknowledge their ontological undecidability. Realism, by bringing that which might not have happened to full textual presence, can be accused of constructing a reality that never really was. The uncanny experience produced by Mantel's text can be said to do the opposite. It allows the life writer to articulate the experience of loss: the past and other people as things that are inevitably lost, and also the process of writing about them as involving further loss (because the text inevitably constructs them as something other). Textual presence has to be spectral because it is articulating this loss. The haunted house acts as a figure for this double loss; the first chapter is entitled 'A Second Home', and does refer to Mantel's literal second home, a holiday cottage in Norfolk, but equally it refers to the second home of language in which the cottage becomes a haunted house. The ghost is the figure that is used to articulate the space that is the real as it is constructed by language; what James Donald, in his discussion of the uncanny experience of modern physical existence, describes as, 'the uneasy space between the physical and the imaginary' (Donald cited in Collins and Jervis, 2008: 5). Mantel uses the haunted house to articulate this 'space' between the physical and its memory or imagining in language throughout the text. She returns to the difficulty of finding an adequate form for writing about the personal past thus:

> Writing about your past is like blundering through your house with the lights fused, a hand flailing for points of reference. You locate the stolid wardrobe, and its door swings open at your touch, opening on the cavern of darkness within. Your hand touches glass, you think it is a mirror, but it is the window. There are obstacles to bump and trip you, but what is more disconcerting is a sudden empty space, where you can't find a handhold and you know that you are stranded in the dark. (Mantel, 2003/2004: 167)

The disconcerting 'sudden empty space' where memory fails is the haunted house of memoir at its most spectral. The archival enterprise of memoir fails at this point because 'you are stranded in the dark', and this being 'stranded in the dark' is all that you can record, unless you make recourse to the strategies of realism and 'make something up' in order to fill those gaps of memory. But the inclusion of the 'empty space' does something radical to the archival record. It articulates a liminal point of narrative; a point that cannot *fully and truthfully* be in the narrative, because there is no way of accessing the loss without turning it into something that never was. The 'sudden empty space' is a moment where the text, in Renza's terms, 'inhibits its ostensible project of self-representation'. Mantel could have filled this space but chooses to leave herself and her readers 'stranded in the dark', in order to give the textual experience of the inaccessible past.

It is for this ability to open up the process of turning experience into discourse, and particularly to examine memory as an archive of the lost past, that memoir can claim to be an ethical form of truth telling. In becoming archons of this undecidable archive where that which is lost in the past can only be archived as a spectre or ghost, writers such as Mantel articulate the complex relationship between a text and its referential world. Ghosts of this referential world are what these texts produce, because that is all texts ever do (most just don't acknowledge or foreground this). By making the ghost a central figure these texts do acknowledge this. Mantel ends her text by sitting down to tea with her dead relatives in her childhood home and articulates her writerly relationship to them: 'I will always look after you I want to say, however long you have been gone. I will always feed you, and try to keep you entertained; and you must do the same for me' (Mantel, 2003/2004: 252). For a writer to 'look after' her dead relatives necessarily involves an ethical consideration of how to translate a past material existence into textual presence. Mantel the author positions herself as a kind of literary medium, through whom the dead might speak.[3]

This develops further the ethical project of such memoirs. As Mantel's final figure, where she promises to 'look after' her dead relatives in their second spectral home of language, suggests, memoir can open up questions about the process of writing about others. Looking after the dead, and giving them a textual afterlife can be perceived as a way of putting them onto the historical record; making their lives count. But it also raises the question of how this can, ethically, be achieved.

Blake Morrison's *And when did you last see your father?* and Paul Morley's *Nothing* both have the same dilemma; how can someone who has died, who was once present but now no longer exists materially, be given textual presence? They seem to offer opposing strategies; whereas Morley highlights the failure of realism, Morrison begins with a performance of it, which seems to re-present his living father as he really was. He describes an incident from his childhood. In the present tense, Morrison takes readers back to a family outing to a motor racing event in 1959. It is evoked in sensory detail:

> The roof of our Alvis is down, the sun beating on to the leather upholstery, the chrome, the picnic basket. The hood is folded and pleated into the mysterious crevice between the boot and the narrow back seat where my sister and I are scrunched together as usual. (Morrison, 1993–2006: 10)

The strong and exact verbs, 'beating', 'folded and pleated' and 'scrunched', coupled with the present tense, are used to take readers into the experience that is perceived to be directly behind the language. There is no sense that this is merely a textual performance. Morrison goes on to recount dialogue between his parents and his father and a racecourse steward with the appearance of precise verisimilitude. Again there is no indication that this is an imaginative reconstruction, using fictional details to give a sense of what surely the adult Morrison cannot remember with such precision of his nine-year-old self. Instead the textual reconstruction of this event, with his father's central and absolute presence in it – 'Our father is on his own. He is not with us, this bullying, shaming undemocratic cheat' (Morrison, 1993–2006: 11) – is presented as evidence of his identity: 'This is the way it was with my father' (Morrison, 1993–2006: 13).

Counter to this, Morley presents the impossibility of re-presenting his father thus. For him realism is an empty strategy, with nothing behind it, as he suggests ways that he could have written about his father, presenting him as a 'living' textual character:

> He crunched with feeling on a mouthful of cornflakes and let the intense sweetness cascade through his body with a chill that was thrilling and intimate ... One chapter included a conversation I had with my father over a pint of bitter in a pub. (The conversation was imaginary, and so was the pint of bitter. We never had a drink in a pub.) At one point I pretended that he'd said to me: 'I agree that it is very important to leave an incomplete image of oneself.' (Morley, 2000: 18)

The exaggerated parody of the sensory language to evoke his father's eating highlights the falsity of such a strategy to bring his father into the text. The strong verbs and adjectives have the opposite effect to Morrison's use of sensory language. With Morley there is a clear indication that this is a textual trick; there is no real experience behind the linguistic performance. It is a simulacrum. The whole notion of textual presence is thus undermined, leaving Morley with the problem of how to write about that which has disappeared, his father, of whom he only has 'an incomplete image'. Like Mantel's 'sudden empty space' this gives textual presence to a moment of inhibition. Morley's father is a ghost, 'an incomplete image' because he cannot translate him into language. What the text does is to articulate the impossibility of having a complete image of a person.

This absolute textual presence of Morrison's father seems to be at odds with the argument being made here about memoir and the spectral. It is only when viewed in juxtaposition with the rendition of Morrison's dying father, that the use of this fictional strategy is more fully understandable. The memoir was begun as a writer's response to his father's final illness. It is an archive of his father's physical disappearance in death, kept in a journal. The question of the title is centrally concerned with this testimony to a person's disappearance:

> *When did you last see your father?* Was it when they burnt the coffin? Put the lid on it? When he exhaled his last breath? ...When he last thought he might be healthy, before they brought the news? The weeks before he left us, or life left him, were a series of depletions; each day we thought 'he can't get less like himself than this,' and each day he did. I keep trying to find the last moment when he was still unmistakably there in the fullness of his being, *him*. (Morrison, 1993–2006: 203)

The text archives these depletions to the final point of disappearance; it is about the shift from presence to absence. Morrison scrutinizes in detail the process of his father's death and his own response to it. When his father dies he examines, textually, in minute detail, the dead body. He presents his father's dead body, 'in the flesh', not wanting to let go of it:

> [A]nd we lift his head and remove some of the pillows from under it ... and draw the covers up to his chest – why would anyone, except in the movies, draw them over the head, and shut out before time what will soon be unseeable forever? (Morrison, 1993–2006: 149)

It is a moment that Derrida might articulate as, 'the instant when the printed archive is yet to be detached from the primary impression in its singular, irreproducible, and archaic origin' (Derrida, 1996: 97–8). The text is enacting its own process of turning material flesh into textual trace. It is in contrast to this idea of the dead person as becoming 'unseeable forever' that the effect of the textual presence of his remembered living father is made. Morrison's afterword to the 2006 edition of the book is interesting in this regard. It is after his father's death; after his careful recording of that death that he begins to write down his memories of his living father: 'The only solace came from childhood memories of my father in rude health' (Morrison, 2006: 220). This is the only way in which that which has become 'unseeable forever' can be brought back into view. The absolute textual presence of his remembered/imagined father is haunted from the beginning by the loss of his father as a physical presence. In searching for a name for this kind of text Morrison suggests that it could be termed as 'Death Writing' (Morrison, 2006: 220). Writing narratives about the dead, 'told by a reliable narrator' (Morrison, 2006: 223), gives them an 'afterlife' (Morrison, 2006: 229) that they would not have if they were not written about. He is aware, in other words, that he is conjuring ghosts. The text is standing in for the 'body' of the lost dead person as with Mantel and Morley. This is even more starkly articulated in his later book, *As if*, where he briefly returns to memories of his dying father. Instead of the textually confident, 'This is the way it was with my father', he describes the experience of returning to his derelict childhood home; a home that he can only describe as haunted as he walks through it 'like a ghost of my own past':

> Its decay is like my father on his deathbed: the lath bones showing through plaster, the ruined innards, the boarded-up eyes. Even its emptiness seems apt: room for imagining, for projecting memory's cine on the blank walls.' (Morrison, 1997: 119)

Here Morrison has moved more fully from realism, to the spectral, where all that the memoir can conjure is a ghost of the past; not 'the thing itself', but the projections of 'memory's cine'.

The issues raised here have shaped the turn to the spectral in my own memoir. Specifically the spectral provided a means for me to both contribute to a textual engagement with the historical events of the Moors murders, and to challenge accounts of those events in which realism is used to present an impression of historical accuracy. Emlyn Williams' *Beyond Belief* (1967) exemplifies this use of realism, through which the Moors murders have been given a particular narrative shape, as an archetypal story of innocence and evil. It is through this narrative that 'the thing itself', the real murders, is understood. I have reproduced here a preface to a longer memoir, *Archives and Ghosts,* which articulates my reasons for wanting to make a spectral engagement with a historical narrative and what this might achieve as a strategy for historical engagement more generally. The preface is called 'Looking for my Dad'.

Looking for my Dad

I looked for him twice ... The second time I looked for him was in May 2006. He had been dead for nearly two and a half years. I wasn't going to, but at the last moment I decided to watch *See No Evil,* Granada Television's drama about the Moors murders, even though I knew I wouldn't find him there either. The first dramatic account that took head on one of the most notorious post-war British murder narratives; it was being screened forty years after Ian Brady and Myra Hindley's convictions for the murders of John Kilbride, Lesley Ann Downey and Edward Evans. There had been a whole corpus of books about the case and dramas that referred to it previously, but no dramatic production that aimed at a full reconstruction. This time lag is telling: it took forty years for the story to be thought safe enough for a direct dramatic representation; but even after forty years it was still potent enough to be worth dramatizing. The names of Brady and Hindley are supposed to haunt all of us who were children in the late

1960s; particularly in the North West. Their abduction of children from the streets of East Manchester, murder for sexual pleasure and the burial of their bodies on the Yorkshire Moors is one of those stories we are supposed to just 'know'; the stuff of cultural myth. We don't have to be told that they were evil incarnate, we can still see it in the faces in their arrest photographs.

Except, I have to admit, I was not familiar with the story, not that familiar anyway; it wasn't something I just 'knew'. It was a story that was always treated with suspicion in our house, not because my parents didn't believe Brady and Hindley guilty of the crimes for which they were convicted, but because they suspected the motives of those who perpetrated the myth, those who set Brady and Hindley up as eternal, unequivocal figures of hate. They had their reasons. My parents were probation officers; they had moved to Manchester in the early 1960s to join its probation service. Their Moors murders narrative started there, in Manchester, in the Gorton Probation Office, where my dad was assigned David Smith as a juvenile client. And it is David Smith's name, not Brady or Hindley's that haunted my childhood. Aged seventeen, he witnessed Brady and Hindley's final murder and reported it to the police, which I suppose makes him the first Moors murders author. It was his testimony that brought the whole thing to light and convicted Brady and Hindley.

It also defined his subsequent life. Married to Hindley's sister, Maureen, befriended by Brady and already with a criminal record for violence, doubt was always cast (not least by Brady and Hindley, themselves, at their trial) about his role in the murder of Edward Evans. Although his evidence gave him immunity from prosecution, it didn't give him immunity from public or media speculation and hatred. So my parents' Moors murders narrative was not about the fundamental evil of Brady and Hindley, but was embedded in an understanding of a different kind of violence; the kind of violence that is an everyday, endemic part of industrial poverty. It was the kind of violence that goes on in families and in communities; not a matter of good and evil, but one possible response to your situation, just part of the messy, complicated way life is. It was the kind of violence that, if you believe Emlyn Williams in *Beyond Belief*, the ur-text of Moors murders narratives, did not exist on the streets of Manchester in the 1960s, until Ian Brady and Myra Hindley stepped out on them. My parents' Moors murders narrative was about how you help David Smith survive its impact on his life; how you help him survive when he gets sent to prison because he's got into a fight with someone over his part in them, when his wife puts their children into care because she can't cope on her own, when his life fractures and falls apart because it can't escape from the myth he's inadvertently helped create, when, frightened, young and implicated, he reported an act of horrific brutality to the police.

So, even though my dad had been researched to be a character in *See No Evil*, even though it was Smith who put the researchers in touch with him, I knew he had requested that no character be based on him. He hadn't wanted to be a part of the story. I wouldn't find him there. I don't know if his decision was based on that suspicion of Moors murders narratives, the fear that he might become a bit part in their mythology. He was a very selfless man, my dad; he might just have balked at the idea of any dramatic representation, at being a 'character' of any kind. *See No Evil* was screened in two parts, shown over consecutive nights. When I started watching I tried to imagine where, if he had allowed it, my dad might have appeared; what kind of role he would have been given. I tried to conjure his figure; but all I could manage was a suited figure, its back to the camera, just moving out of shot. It was a stupid and pointless thing to do. He wasn't there; this wasn't 'what really happened'. It was a story put together to give a sense of the reality that couldn't possibly be reconstructed, because it was too complicated, too embedded in other stories, involved too many other people, who, like my dad, weren't represented.

By the end of the second part, it was exactly this sense of the loss from the narrative that was conveyed. It had stopped being the story of Brady and Hindley. Even though the drama was marketed as their story (the DVD subsequently sold in a box with a picture of Maxine Peake, all flinty eyes, peroxide hair and shadowed cheekbones, as Myra in her arrest photograph), it became that of David and Maureen Smith. Joanne Froggat as Maureen, the inverse of Myra, with darkened hair, huge pools of eyes and washed away face, is used to ask this question: how can you be the sister of evil incarnate? What can you do in the face of such a powerful narrative, a narrative that completely subsumes your identity? The drama ends in the early 1970s. David Smith, after his prison sentence, is living with his father, raising his three sons as a single parent. Maureen returns and they try to put their family back together again, but she looks at her children fearfully with those enormous eyes and, on a pretext, leaves the house. The audience knows she can't hack it; can't be a mother. As she walks away her character fades completely out of the shot, leaving an empty street.

I don't know if this is a truthful representation, something that really happened; Maureen Smith died in 1981 so can't give her version of events. But there is a kind of truth in that shot of a woman disappearing. Maureen Smith's is a story that can't be told. How can she compete with the Moors murders? All she can do is disappear, walk away and fade out of shot leaving you on an empty street. There's no resolution; just the loss of someone who falls outside the historical record, walks away from the story, keeps herself out because she can't be a part of it. What else can you do if you're Myra Hindley's sister? What case can you make against the absolute cultural presence, the narrative clarity of that photograph, that story? How can you say that was not the way it was? You're Myra Hindley's sister, for God's sake, and everybody knows what she was like. What can you do, except disappear?

So, I'm left with a conundrum; like Maureen Smith, my dad has disappeared. All I can find is his absence from a narrative of which he was undoubtedly a part. He was, somehow 'in' the Moors murders. But the story carries on without him, as if he never existed. He has faded out of shot and I'm left on an empty street. How can I bring him back, let people know that he was there, that his presence changes the whole thing, without turning him into a character who never existed, in a story that never happened?

The spectral memoir is used here as a mode that can wrest power away from realist historical texts that impose narrative certainty and purport to give readers 'the thing itself', complete and undeformed, as it was in life. A spectral engagement acknowledges instead that texts can only haunt the past, never master it; that 'the thing itself' has to be in quotation marks because it is always a textual conjuring of something that would otherwise be 'unseeable forever'. As a writer of auto/biography, the spectral is a powerful form through which to articulate the dual position of the author as both inside and outside the text; 'simultaneously a socially responsible real person, and the producer of a discourse' (Lejeune, 1982: 200) Rather than a model of history as mastery of the past, the spectral memoir offers a model of an ongoing process of textual haunting, which allows a critical examination of the discursive dimensions of lived experience. The ghost story is an ethical discourse of a socially responsible person.

Notes

1 Philippe Lejeune (1982) and Paul John Eakin (2008) have both emphasized the specific contract that auto/biography must establish with its readers in terms of the textual relationship to its referential 'outside'. As Eakin (2008: 20) argues, 'readers expect autobiographers to exhibit some basic respect for the truth of their lives'.

2 For the ongoing debate about testimonio as a life-writing form and political intervention see Beverley (2004).

3 Consideration of Mantel as a kind of literary psychic or medium is interesting in relation to her novel *Beyond Black* (2005), in which the central character is a medium. Her ability to converse with dead is used as a textual strategy to address how the past haunts the present.

References

Beverley, J. (2004) *Testimonio: on the Politics of Truth*. Minneapolis: University of Minnesota Press.

Brooke-Rose, C. (1981) *A Rhetoric of the Unreal: Studies in Narrative and Structure Especially of the Fantastic*. Cambridge: Cambridge University Press.

Collins, J. and Jervis, J. (eds) (2008) *Uncanny Modernity*. Basingstoke: Palgrave Macmillan.

Derrida, J. (1994) *Specters of Marx*, trans. Peggy Kamuf. New York: Routledge.

Derrida, J. (1996) *Archive Fever*, trans by Eric Prenowitz. Chicago, IL: The Chicago University Press.

Eakin, P.J. (2008) *Living Autobiographically: How We Create Identity in Narrative*. Ithaca, NY: Cornell University Press.
Lauritzen, P. (2004) 'Arguing with Life Stories: The Case of Rigoberta Menchú', in P.J. Eakin (ed.) *The Ethics of Life Writing*, pp. 19–40. Ithaca, NY: Cornell University Press.
Lejeune, P. (1982) 'The Autobiographical Contract', in T. Todorov (ed.) *French Literary Theory Today: A Reader*, pp. 190–230. Cambridge: Cambridge University Press.
Mantel, H. (2003/2004) *Giving up the Ghost*. London: Harper Perennial.
Mantel, H. (2005) *Beyond Black*. London: Harper Perennial.
Menchú, R. (1984–94) *I Rigoberta Menchú: An Indian Woman in Guatemala*, ed. Elisabeth Burgos-Debray, trans. by Ann Wright. London: Verso.
Morley, P. (2000) *Nothing*. London: Faber & Faber.
Morrison, B. (1993–2006) *And when did you last see your Father?* London: Granta.
Morrison, B. (2006) Afterword, in *And when did you last see your Father?* London: Granta.
Morrison, B. (1997) *As If*. London: Granta.
Pleasance, H. (2011) 'Lost Children, the Moors & Evil Monsters: the photographic story of the Moors murders', *Image [&] Narrative* 12(4): 18–38, accessed May 2012, http://www.imageandnarrative.be/index.php/imagenarrative/issue/view/15
Renza, L.A. (1980) 'The Veto of the Imagination: A Theory of Autobiographical Form', in J. Olney (ed.) *Autobiography: Essays Theoretical and Critical*, pp. 268–95. Princeton, NJ: Princeton University Press.
Tagg, J. (1988) *The Burden of Representation, Essays on Photographies and Histories*. Basingstoke: Palgrave Macmillan.
Williams, E. (1967–92) *Beyond Belief*. London: Pan.

'One doesn't have much but oneself'
Christopher Isherwood's Investigation into Identity and the Manipulation of Form in *The Memorial*

Rebecca Gordon Stewart

Christopher Isherwood's lifelong friend Stephen Spender wrote that:

> Christopher's genius is to be entirely Christopher, and yet, at the same time to act out roles, as Chris, Mr. Issyvoo, and someone who calls himself 'I,' and this juggling of masks and personae has fascinated thousands of readers. (Spender, 1980: 11)

Spender's assertion implies that there is some kind of authentic Christopher, who fascinates the reader by continuously acting out roles. However, as a reader (as distinct from those who knew Isherwood as a friend) I can only have access to these 'roles', and the impression gained from these is that there is a multiplicity of 'selves', which change in time, change as self-images shift, change as intellectual preoccupations shift, but which also change as a function of literary mode. What makes Isherwood's self-exploration and self-presentation interesting is that he appears to vary literary kinds and modes deliberately in order to create the many 'selves' that are comprehended in the name Christopher Isherwood. That all of Isherwood's characters are 'entirely Christopher' is clearly undermined by the fact that even the selves who are called 'I' are not identical; Isherwood writes himself in a way that makes him seem multiform.

Isherwood's career spanned almost seven decades, and in that time he wrote many novels, screenplays, short stories, novellas and 'autobiographical' works. The narrators and male protagonists of these works have indeed 'fascinated' readers, but they have also infuriated them, tempting them with an apparent insight into Isherwood's personal and private life, while all the time withholding the vital *clef* to his seeming *roman*. Blurring the distinction between autobiography and fiction, Isherwood created and re-created his fictional and indeed at times fantastical imagined world, forming a literary mythology in which the distinctions between 'fact' and 'fiction' are blurred, and deliberately confused.

Samuel Hynes argues that the 'writer of an autobiography is constructing a Myth of Himself, which by imposing shape and selection upon the past will explain his present existence' (Hynes, 1976: 322). This is true, but for Isherwood it is true of every work: every work imposes its own shape upon the past. Isherwood represents a version of self in each of his writings, and in each, whether 'fiction' or 'non-fiction', he creates another idea or conceptualization of Christopher. Each of Isherwood's works is another self-definition, another effort in self-creation. In his literature, the individual is defined by the writing process; Isherwood is consistently engaging with the idea that the self is something sculpted in words, rather than something that pre-exists, as can be seen in the manner in which he manipulates the forms he employs, and the ways in which he does this determine the self that is dramatized in his writing.

Manipulation of the forms of autobiography and intellectual strategies for the representation of self within *The Memorial*

Christopher Isherwood manipulates his ever-evolving ideas of self to shape not only his works that are presented as autobiography (those narrated by Christopher), but also the entire body of his work, which includes his early novels *All the Conspirators* (1928) and *The Memorial*

(1932), both of which are narrated by a third person narrator and presented as fictional. Although Isherwood has not fully come to terms with the representation of self as both subject and object as he would later with the introduction of his namesake protagonist, both of these early books still act as a self-presentation. Indeed, by removing his own name from these early narratives, Isherwood is arguably able to be more frank than his self-imaged Christopher character ever could.

A preliminary analysis of these early novels leads to an understanding that *All the Conspirators* and *The Memorial* are undeniably autobiographical novels. Both books focus ostensibly on a young male protagonist, Philip Lindsay and Eric Vernon respectively, and these young men bear an overwhelming resemblance to their author, and plots mirror events in Isherwood's own life.[1] Isherwood is writing about his 'past', through semi-fictionalized characters that bear resemblance to himself as he 'was', he 'is' and he 'may be', or at least how he presents others to perceive him. It is, however, only with hindsight that readers are able to approach these narratives as 'autobiographical': the third person narrator, unlike the first person namesake narrator adopted by Isherwood in so many of his subsequent books, superficially conceals any relationship between narrator and author.

However, rather than relying solely on being able to compare the lives of the characters with their author, it is the manner in which Isherwood focuses on autobiographical debates that leads to an understanding that these early novels are part of Isherwood's mythologizing process. *The Memorial* in particular represents a consciously-adopted strategy for self-exploration. Although *The Memorial* was not specifically written as autobiography, the manner in which Isherwood manipulates the form of this early novel helps in his construction of a literary self.

In the first instance, the form of *The Memorial* can be linked to the autobiographical act of self-understanding and self-analysis. The books of this novel are nonlinear: Book One opens in 1928, going back in Book Two to 1920, progressing to 1925 in the third book, with the final book set in 1929. Although the fractured narrative could be compared to the modernist experiments of the early twentieth century, the distorted chronology of *The Memorial* is more intimately related to Isherwood's representation and analysis of the self.

The manner in which Eric and indeed all the characters of *The Memorial* are narrated in a nonlinear manner highlights Isherwood's understanding and adoption of autobiographical and Freudian themes. In the first instance, Eric's neuroses are highlighted and undeniably linked to this character's own unsettled childhood.[2] The way that the 'adult' Eric is narrated in Book One, which shifts to the narrative of the undeniably neurotic Edward Blake before reverting back into childhood as Lily Vernon talks of her son, highlights Isherwood's Freudian emphasis on the link between neurosis and the effects of parentage and childhood. The manner in which Isherwood juxtaposes Eric's adulthood with his childhood highlights their connection, and Isherwood clearly demonstrates that Eric's 'failures' in young adulthood are fundamentally linked to his childhood, with particular stress being put on the death of his father and the figurative loss of his mother.

Second, the splintered timescale also emphasises that the representation and indeed understanding of 'self' is not a linear progression. What is presented in writing is not a 'life-as-lived'; instead, the understanding of self that is written is linked only to the present-day man, who can cross time and relate parts of his life as he wishes. Whether 'intentional' or not, all authors of self manipulate their 'life-stories' in order to represent the mythologies of the present-day self. Therefore, by adopting this non-linear structure for his novel, Isherwood attempts to project a legend of 'self' that is all about the present, rather than an 'as it happens' progressive narrative.

Furthermore, each element of the book is clearly narrated from the point of view of different characters. Each chapter is representative of a viewpoint, which 'is always passed on by touch, like the baton in a relay race, from one character to another who then takes over the narration' (Geherin, 2001: 75). This limits the narrative and emphasizes the subjectivity of the different accounts, thus highlighting the perception that all narratives are defective and distorted by human memory.

Although it may seem paradoxical to argue the idea that a piece of literature featuring multiple narrative voices is indicative of a representation of self, and by implication the artist, it is this emphasis on perspective that focuses all parts of the book on the question of self: in *The Memorial* Isherwood begins to analyse the manner in which action is less vital than the experiences and visions of the individual. However random elements of this work may seem, the circular way in which the narrative continually returns to the point of view of these fixed characters binds this novel together and focuses on the individual above the action or the plot. In *The Memorial,* Isherwood concentrates on the 'everyday', the 'believable' and, perhaps most vitally, the 'authentic', which is undeniably vital to autobiography. It is his concentration on the representation of human experience that leads to a reading of *The Memorial* as a realistic novel, which, according to Bernard J. Paris, has 'two kinds of minds [...] that can be studied in psychological terms; they are the minds of the implied authors and the minds of the leading characters' (Paris, 1974: 1).

Isherwood, rather than distancing the implied author self from the leading characters, creates a connection between them, and initiates his analytical strategy of writing himself in order to understand himself, which is consistently examined in relation to themes of childhood and heredity. Although there are numerous principal characters within this novel, Eric and Edward, with their alliterative names, represent clearly Isherwood's constructed self and take on the shared role of protagonist: these dual characters symbolize the author as he sees himself and as he fears he will become. Furthermore, both of these characters are seen in direct contrast to Richard Vernon, Eric's father, and hence Isherwood seems to compare himself to his own father, Frank. Eric, Edward and Isherwood all stand for Isherwood's Truly Weak Man.[3]

Isherwood does not appear to have a theory of selfhood, but his writings are permeated with an awareness of the psychoanalytical teachings of Sigmund Freud, who he was greatly influenced by. However, this is not a psychoanalytical reading of *The Memorial*; rather, it is an examination of the way the teachings of Freud are manipulated by Isherwood as he explores different images and concepts of himself, in particular with regard to his own great quest: the search for a self that is mature and can move away from the paranoia of the Truly Weak Man.

This quest relates to the manner in which Isherwood writes and creates a self in reference to the psychoanalytical analysis of the relationships between fathers and sons, and indeed mothers and sons. Freud's own psychoanalytical theories emphasize that 'the chief part in the mental lives of children [...] is played by the parents' (Freud, 1900/2001: 260), and throughout his writing Isherwood repeatedly deals with parentage and heredity. In Freudian psychology the act of 'remembering' that is required for life-writing is connected to the 'childhood drama of love, hate and jealousy in relation to one's parents' (Anderson, 2001: 61). The critic Linda Anderson focuses on the manner in which autobiographers concentrate on the father in their writing; in connection with two autobiographies that she examines she offers the hypothesis that 'autobiographical subjects attempt to rediscover a relationship to a father who has been largely absent from their childhood' (Anderson, 2001: 119). A number of Isherwood's books can be categorized clearly as 'son novels'. In *The Memorial* this can be witnessed in the manner in which the protagonist Eric 'wrenches' himself away from the authority of his father, or at least the image of the father as presented by The Others.[4]

After his father's death in WWI, when Isherwood was only eleven-years old, the traditional patriarchal figure of authority was removed. Isherwood attempts in his writing not only to 'rediscover' a relationship with Frank Isherwood, which is what Anderson's theory proposes, but also to consider the effects of his loss, which includes an analysis of his rebellion against the Mother and his search for surrogates. The effect of his loss on his literary self constitutes the focus of Isherwood's writing. The 'autobiographical' act as performed by Isherwood is ostensibly an analytical act.

Furthermore, Isherwood engages with autobiographical and Freudian debates not only to present, but also to form a version of 'I' that is affected by, but does not always include, a father. This links directly to the manner in which Isherwood's main protagonists analyse themselves in direct reference to an inferiority, which articulates their regret that they were not old enough to have fought in the war that killed Isherwood's father. This can be seen for example in the homoeroticized mock heroics of his juvenilia piece 'Gems of Belgian Architecture'; the role of family in the act of stifling the artistic son in his first published novel *All the Conspirators*; and the representation of Christopher's reactions to the 'terror of War', which does not deal with the loss of the father directly, but is instead generalized in *Lions and Shadows*.

Isherwood's emphasis on the mental aspects of his male characters within *The Memorial* focuses his writing on Freudian psychoanalytical debates. These neuroses are directly associated to the characters' childhood and the obscurer aspects of mental activity. Isherwood seems consistently to be compelled to write his characters from the position that there is some psychological cause, which is linked to their childhood and their relationships with their parents, for their adult psychoses, which can be seen in particular in an examination of the two main protagonists that are most clearly representative of Isherwood's fictionalized self: Eric and Edward.

In the creation of Eric, Isherwood clearly adopts Freudian language and concepts. Eric's narrative is linked to theories such as narcissism and the Oedipus complex; the fractured narrative assimilates Eric's later paranoia and neuroses to his childhood. The oedipal hatred of the father, which is connected to the jealousy of the affection the father receives from the mother, leads to a desire to depose the father. For Eric, this has already been achieved: Richard has been killed in WWI. According to Freudian theory, Eric's adversary has been removed and he should now be free to enjoy his mother's affection.

As with Hamlet, however, whom Freud himself analysed with regard to the Oedipus complex, the Mother's exclusive love that Eric so craves is removed. In *The Memorial,* Lily Vernon's own nostalgia and craving to recreate the past, a time when Richard was still alive, means that Eric remains second to Richard in his mother's eyes. It is this fundamentally Freudian basis to Eric's character that leads to an understanding of all of his character flaws. For example, Eric's childhood feelings of inadequacy stem from the idea that, unlike his father, he had been unable to prove himself in WWI, which indisputably is portrayed as stemming from Lily's representation of what Eric's father had been: Lily links father and son, with particular reference to Eric's lesser status in her mind (*Memorial,* p. 59), and it is this loss of maternal affection that leads Eric into his quest to emulate his father. Eric clearly attempts to please his mother and presents an external desire to be *like* Richard; in Books One and Two of *The Memorial,* which deal with Eric's failed university career and childhood respectively, the emphasis is placed on how Eric's life-choices copy what his mother and The Others tell him his father would have done if he had been 'allowed' to live.

However, there remains an emphasis on rebellion within *The Memorial* (albeit one that ostensibly fails), and the desire to revolt against the image of Hero-Father is highlighted by the way that Eric deals with his father's death. There is a shift to Eric's voice as he 'remembers' hearing the news: 'Eric was very, very sorry to hear that his father had been killed' (*Memorial,* pp. 130-1). This free indirect speech with a repetition of 'very' echoes the words of The Others; it is, however, the discomfort he feels at boarding school that Eric focuses on, thus demonstrating ambivalence to the news of his father's death, an ambivalence that relates to Freud's analysis of the way in which a son deals with a father's death.

In *The Ego and the Id,* Freud discusses a boy's 'ambivalent attitude to his father' (Freud, 1923/2001: 32), which is continued in his case study of 'The Rat Man' (1909/2001). The contrast between love and loathing in Freud's analysis of the Rat Man, especially the way in which this neurotic deals with the death of his father by creating a ghost-father that loves on 'as a frightening or punishing paternal image' (Thurschwell, 2000: 65), is particularly prevalent when discussing the images present within *The Memorial.* Although Richard is absent from his life, he continually haunts Eric as an authority figure who threatens, even in death, to punish Eric for his treatment of his mother: 'Suppose Father were to come back from the grave [...] This was one of Eric's nightmares' (*Memorial,* p. 179). Freud argued that for the sufferer of paranoia and neuroses, the authority figure of the father, even after his death, remains frightening and haunts his son. Thus the judgement that Eric both fears and rebels against is essentially Freudian; his neuroses are consistently linked to the image of the father and Isherwood personalizes these classical themes and uses them as the basis of his own ideology of self.

The personalizing of the general Freudian themes can also be seen in Isherwood's paradoxical concepts of manhood. In *The Memorial,* the image of The Hero-Father, Richard, is placed in polar opposition to the son of the War-Hero, Eric. In *Lions and Shadows,* Isherwood shifts the emphasis of his description of paranoia from 'father' (which is the situation in *The Memorial*) towards what is described in *Lions and Shadows* as Christopher's 'obsession' with and paranoia regarding his 'complex terrors' of War (*Lions and Shadows,* pp. 55-6). And within *Lions and Shadows* he discusses the manner in which he created *The Memorial.* In what is a mythologized examination of his earlier writing he indicates that this novel was intended to discuss his own personal fear regarding the War:

> It was to be about war: not the War itself, but the effect of the idea of 'War' on my generation. It was to give expression, at last, to my own 'War' complex (*Lions and Shadows,* 236).

Within this 'autobiographical' exploration of his reasons behind the creation of 'an epic disguised as a drawing-room comedy' (Isherwood, 1938: 236), Isherwood completely removes his father's death, and instead the paranoia vented by war is a general condition that 'stands for' the hero's attitude to 'the father'. However, *The Memorial,* more than any other of his literary creations prior to the biography of his parents, *Kathleen and Frank,* narrates the 'real' father as well as the 'surrogate' father. The explanations offered in *Lions and Shadows* help in an understanding of the way in which Isherwood was representing himself in his earlier novel: they expound the psychological themes of *The Memorial* that make up his literary ideology.

Intrinsically linked to the manner in which Isherwood writes of male characters in his books generally, and of surrogate fathers and the terrors of War specifically, is the analysis of his own ideas of heroism. In *Lions and Shadows,* Isherwood directly examines his own concepts of strength in his paradoxical classification of the Truly Strong Man and the Truly Weak Man. The terminology that Isherwood adopts as part of his theory on heroics is based on Eugen Bleuler's discussion of paranoia in his work *Textbook of Psychiatry* (1924/1951), which Isherwood refers to within *Lions and Shadows* (p. 163).[5] In Bleuler's assessment of an engineer named Wagner, whom he classes as suffering from delusions of persecution, the themes of strength and weakness are presented through self-analysis performed by the patient. Wagner sees and presents his own weakness in direct contrast to what he imagines as the 'truly strong':

> The signs of the truly strong are repose and good-will. The strong man, about whom we palaver in our literature, does not exist. [...] The strong individuals are those who without any fuss do their duty. These have neither the time nor the occasion to throw themselves into a pose and try to be something great. (Bleuler, 1924/1951: 531)

Wagner argues that the conventional hero is in actuality an unachievable myth-like figure.

The traditions of heroics are in Wagner's own mind linked to his psychoses; the expectations placed on young males by society are what have led him to his failures and paranoia. Additionally, he would only be able to escape his 'illness' if he was 'strong' in the manner that is in polar opposition to the conventional ideas of strength and heroics. This is essential to understanding the ideological stance of the principal characters of *The Memorial*.

This paradoxical emphasis on non-action is central to Isherwood's representation of the ideal male and is most clearly evident in an analysis of Richard Vernon as representative of Frank Isherwood. Richard can be clearly seen as becoming split into two characters, a literary tool that Isherwood often manipulated: on the one hand he is the Hero–Father, the ghost that haunts Eric's childhood, which affects this literary self through adolescence into adulthood, and on the other hand, he is also the mythological anti-heroic hero, the Truly Strong Man. Indeed, Richard appears to be the only character within this novel that is genuinely representative of the Truly Strong Man.

Engaging with how the Truly Strong Man is presented in *Lions and Shadows*, a comparison can be made with the description of Richard in *The Memorial*. Isherwood (1938: 163) sees the Truly Strong Man as an ideal and he emphasizes that it is the Strong Man that does not need to leave his 'comfortable home in the snowstorm to climb the impossible glacier'. Looking at the way that Richard is described by Edward in *The Memorial*, he stresses strong versus weak as he idolizes his friend:

> Richard's strength and calm made him conscious of his own weakness. [...] Richard had no need to give proofs of his courage, to assert the strength of his will [...] he did not have to fight and boast. He was brave – unnecessary for him to climb the chapel roof or swim the river in clothes to win a shilling bet. (*Memorial*, p. 116)

Written from Edward's point of view, it is evident that Edward, like Isherwood's represented self in *Lions and Shadows* and Bleuler's patient Wagner, 'understands' that the heroics as emphasized by literature and society are not real, that it is the calm and balanced man that is Strong. However, both Edward and Christopher are unable to take this self-analysis and understanding to the next level of self-medication; despite their ability to view their own flaws they remain the neurotic hero.

The emphasis on non-action as a trait of the Truly Strong Man is central to the way in which Isherwood's male characters can be analysed. It is the Truly Weak Man who feels he has to travel the dangerous Northwest passage, which directly links to his role as the 'neurotic hero' (Isherwood, 1938: 163). The Test that Isherwood places on his young male protagonists only exists for the Truly Weak Man. As an analysis of Isherwood's multiple self-representations in his early writing is performed and the multiple themes examined, it can be argued that all return to the basic neurosis and paranoia caused by his represented feelings of inadequacies, which are linked to his theories regarding the Truly Weak and Truly Strong Man.

As an orphan of a dead hero, Eric must behave in a certain way; he must conduct himself in a manner that is deemed suitable by other people, especially his mother. By having to live his life as others say his father would have wanted, Eric is reminded that he did not fight in the war and is expected to be eternally grateful to the men who died.

All stories of war remind Eric that he has not faced his Test, and all contribute to his sense of inadequacy. For example, at the memorial service in Book Two, Eric hears the story of the young boy, not even sixteen, who had died for his country. The young Eric is plunged into a feeling of hopelessness. Having been reminded anew the he had not fought in the war, Eric creates a romanticized fantasy regarding The Test and his feelings of inadequacy. The fantasy enters his dreams. As Freud remarks, '*a dream is a (disguised) fulfilment of a (suppressed or repressed) wish*' (Freud, 1900/2001: 160, emphasis in original). Here, the relationship between wish and dream is barely suppressed or disguised

Eric realizes that this is a fantasy that is not only unachievable because the war is over, but also because, in his view, he is a coward, one that, without having been tested, has already failed: 'Yes, I'm a coward all right' (*Memorial*, p. 126). Eric's ideas of self are still entirely limited to the way he perceives himself as a second-rate representative of the son of a war-hero. Although Eric is able to 'see' his own dreams, he is not able to analyse them; his unconscious stops him fully understanding the relevance of his fantasies. Isherwood manipulates Freud's paradox regarding self-understanding. Eric is not able to differentiate between the image presented by others and an actual self-understanding that could have been possible.

Just as Richard is presented as the Truly Strong, Eric is undeniably presented as the Truly Weak, and his fate, unless he should be able to recognize his own failures, not in reference to the Test of the war but to his desire to be tested, is to become Edward. Therefore, while Richard can arguably be seen to be taking on the role of Frank Isherwood, Eric and Edward are representative of Isherwood the implied author – the first as he sees himself and the second as he may become.

Both Eric and Edward are evidently counter-figures to Richard. The final chapter of Book One is narrated from Edward's point of view and the reader is witness to what he wishes to be his final Test. Edward is clearly shown to be the Truly Weak Man, which is seen initially by his obsessions with War and The Test, and finally by his attempted suicide, which is a complete failure: even this he 'mucks up'

(*Memorial,* 50-1). This chapter opens with Edward obviously drunk and with false reason rationalising his own death:

> 'Well,' said Edward [...] 'here I am, you see.' For it had suddenly struck him – how queer; ten years ago I wasn't allowed to come down this road. Now it's allowed again. [...] In 1919 we were going to have bombed Berlin. Mathematically speaking, there's no reason why I shouldn't be dropping a bomb on myself at this very moment. (*Memorial*, p. 46)

Edward's idea of mathematical odds seem strange, but the real point is that he is desperate to be Tested, which must align him with Eric, while at the same time he is endeavouring to emulate Richard with his own death in action. He is both parallel to Eric and a substitute father for him.

Just as the reader is forced to analyse the different narratives of *The Memorial,* Edward faces his own analysis prior to his attempted suicide as he attends a psychiatrist. The incorporation of psychoanalysis within Edward's narrative indicates that he is 'not well'; his need for a psychiatrist is in fact intrinsically linked to War and the idea that he sees himself as a 'failure'. Isherwood once again makes a marked connection between Eric and Edward; both of these characters' neuroses are vitally linked to their feelings of guilt and inadequacy at having survived the war.

The emphasis on psychological regression as a way of understanding the present man is central both to Freudian theory and to psychoanalytic practice, and Isherwood deploys an understanding of this in *The Memorial.* But Isherwood does not solemnly reiterate Freud: his narrative shifts to Edward's own point of view as Edward revisits the latest in a line of visits to psychiatrists:

> But, of course, it had just been like all the others. [...] Questions about early childhood. There was a man Edward had been to see years ago [...] who'd elicited with great triumph that once or twice, in 1917, Edward had as good as run away. He'd faked attacks of rheumatism, got several days' sick-leave. 'And so, you see,' the bright little doctor had explained, 'we're at the root of the whole trouble at last. Subconsciously, you've never forgiven yourself. [...] Think of your splendid

> War record. Everyone must have periods of relapse. We aren't made of iron. There's no disgrace at all. None at all'. (*Memorial*, 48)

The psychiatrist is a light-weight; he does not seem to realize that 'knowing' the problem is not the same thing as confronting it: Edward does have a 'splendid War record', but in his own neurotic mind he has failed to prove himself a man. Both Edward and Eric are haunted by the same thing: when it came to The Test of dying for their country, they 'failed' and Richard 'passed'.

Edward's illness is in fact evidence for his really being a Truly Weak Man. It becomes more and more obvious as the narrative progresses that Edward very much belongs to this group. Back to his childhood, before he achieved his 'immaculate war record', Edward is seen to be psychologically rather than physiologically 'unwell'. Edward's neuroses are seen to have existed in his schooldays; with this, Richard and Edward are shown to be polar opposites while simultaneously reinforcing the idea that Edward and Eric are fundamentally the same. Whereas Richard is able to fit into his school by not caring whether he is judged or not, Edward seems to invite trouble and it is through the imagery of the thriller that Edward's Tests are described: 'He'd never submit, not if they tortured him. He almost hoped they'd try' (*Memorial*, 112). He is obsessed with heroic images, images that adjust to the circumstances of life:

> Edward was going to take life by storm. He admitted no final obstacle, no barriers [...] All that he read, either of heroism or success, he applied at once to himself. Could I do that? Of course. And what's more, I will. [...] Everywhere he saw a challenge. [...] He dared refuse no adventure – horribly frightened as he often was. He would have fought any boy in the school, would have got himself expelled for any offence, rather than admit to being afraid. (*Memorial*, 114)

His obsession with heroism is what makes Edward clearly a Truly Weak Man. The desire to 'escape' is always attributed to the Weak Man, and just as Edward tests himself at school, through the war and by eventually becoming a test pilot, he is constantly unable to see himself as the figure that sits and waits.

The Truly Weak Man is intrinsically interrelated with narratives of travel, often being representative of 'escape' within Isherwood's mythology. Edward can be seen to epitomize the Truly Weak Man in all elements of his life. Indeed, Isherwood is very specific with regard to the manner in which Edward had used travel in order to run away: 'To escape [...] he had travelled. China. South Africa. Brazil. [...] climbed the Alps, been round the coasts of Europe in a small sailing boat [...] to risk his life' (*Memorial*, 122). Not only does Edward use travel as a form of escape, he uses it as a Test of his manliness. Edward's travels are all intrinsically linked to the question posed by Isherwood's Test: 'Are you really a Man?' (*Memorial*, 56).

Having established that Edward, in contrast to Richard, is representative of the Truly Weak Man, I wish to return to the importance that this figure has on Isherwood's self-representation; Eric and Edward are connected by their Weakness. Their relationship is a reflection of 'what is' for Eric and 'what might be'. Eric is looking for a figure to replace Richard in Edward, an act that is destined to failure due to the fact that Edward and Richard are polar opposites, but Edward is also searching for someone to replace Richard, a hero that can make him feel 'genuine humility' once more (*Memorial*, 116). This too is fated to be a failure as Eric and Edward are paralleled throughout this novel. Eric is able to see that Edward is Weak (*Memorial*, 195), and yet he is still drawn towards this character, who it seems may offer him The Test that he has been desperately seeking. Ironically, both Edward and Eric are looking for exactly the same thing: they are both desperately seeking Richard –the father-figure.

Conclusion

An analysis of these male figures demonstrates the manner in which Isherwood narrates himself in reference to interrelated and consistent themes. Within *The Memorial*, he manipulates the novel form in order to present a mythology of self. With a focus on the individual characters, in particular the male characters Eric and Edward, it is not merely the similarities between Eric and Isherwood's biography that leads to a reading of *The Memorial* as autobiographical. Both the formal and intellectual strategies adopted by Isherwood demonstrate the connections and continuities with his later first person narratives. Within *The Memorial,* Isherwood manipulates the idea that role-play is a strategy of self-discovery. Eric is representative of Isherwood and by presenting himself in this imagined role he begins the process of a fictionalized self-analysis and also prepares himself for a more complete one that is continued in *Lions and Shadows.*

Isherwood's manipulation of the autobiographical form generates multiple transformations; however, he is not 'juggling masks' as Stephen Spender suggests, but rather is engaging in a series of strategies for finding and presenting a self, a self that is under constant review by the author. My reformulation here is not an unwitting return to the essentialism of Spender, for the multiple images and the overlapping narratives should be seen as the products of a process of creating a mythology of self. Beyond the self-definitions of each work, he is creating the 'Mythology of Isherwood'.

Notes

1 For example, Brian Finney argues that most of the characters of *The Memorial* 'are recognizably modelled on individuals whom he knew intimately and to whom he had already allotted roles in his private mythology'. He further identifies the models for Isherwood's characters (Finney, 1979: 95-6).

2 David Garrett Izzo comments that this style of writing was prevalent in the early twentieth century, although he does not clearly examine the Freudian implications with regard to Isherwood's own writing within this argument (Izzo, 2005: 271n.77).

3 This phrase is introduced in *Lions and Shadows* (1938).

4 In *Kathleen and Frank,* Isherwood talks of the people that formed what he classes as The Other: this includes teachers, the 'disembodied voices from pulpits, newspapers, books', as well as his own mother (p. 356).

5 Paul Eugen Bleuler was a Swiss psychiatrist who is credited with giving the names 'schizophrenia' and 'autism' to the respective conditions. He initially supported Freud's psychoanalytic practice, but withdrew his support in 1911.

References

Anderson, L. (2001) *Autobiography*. London: Routledge.

Bleuler, E. (1924/1951) *Textbook of Psychiatry*. Trans by A. A. Brill. New York: Dover Publications

Finney, B. (1979) *Christopher Isherwood: A Critical Biography*. London: Faber and Faber.

Freud, S. (1923/2001) *The Ego and the Id*, in *The Standard Edition of the Complete Psychological Works of Sigmund Freud: Volume XIX*, trans. by James Strachey. London: Vintage Press.

Freud, S (1900/2001) *The Interpretation of Dreams (First Part)*, in *The Standard Edition of the Complete Psychological Works of Sigmund Freud: Volume IV*, trans. by James Strachey. London: Vintage Press.

Freud, S. (1909/2001) 'Notes upon a Case of Obsessional Neurosis (Rat Man)', in James Strachey trans) *The Standard Edition of the Complete Psychological Works of Sigmund Freud: Volume X*, pp. 153-318. London: Vintage Press.

Geherin, D.J. (2001) 'An Interview with Christopher Isherwood', in J. Berg and C. Freeman (eds) *Conversations with Christopher Isherwood*, pp. 74-89. Mississippi: University Press of Mississippi.

Hynes, S. (1976) *The Auden Generation: Literature and Politics in England in the 1930s*. London: The Bodley Head.

Isherwood, C. (1928/2000) *All the Conspirators*. London: Vintage.

Isherwood, C. (1939/1992) *Goodbye to Berlin* in *The Berlin Novels*. London: Vintage Random House.

Isherwood, C. (1971/1992) *Kathleen and Frank*. London: Mandarin Paperbacks.

Isherwood, C. (1938/1977) *Lions and Shadows*. New York: New Directions Books.

Isherwood, C. (1932/1988) *The Memorial*. London: Methuen.

Izzo, D. G. (2001) *Christopher Isherwood: His Era, His Gang, and the Legacy of the Truly Strong Man*. Columbia, SC: University of South Carolina Press.

Paris, B J. (1974) *A Psychological Approach to Fiction: Studies in Thackeray, Stendhal, George Eliot, Dostoevsky, and Conrad*. London: Indiana University Press.

Spender, S. (1980) *Letters to Christopher: Stephen Spender's Letters to Christopher Isherwood 1929-1939*, ed. Lee Bartlett. Santa Barbara: Black Sparrow Press.

Thurschwell, P. (2000) *Sigmund Freud*. London: Routledge.
Wilde, A. (1971) *Christopher Isherwood*. New York: Twayne Publishers.

MENNA, MARTHA AND ME
THE POSSIBILITIES OF EPISTOLARY CRITICISM

Rhiannon Marks

Dear Reader,

How are you? I hope that you're well and that you're enjoying the volume so far. I also hope that you don't mind my addressing you directly like this. It might strike you as being rather strange since it goes completely against the conventions of academic writing, doesn't it?

When writing an 'academic' piece there are often expectations on the part of the author and reader alike: that the work is formatted in a specific way and divided neatly into chapters supported by footnotes, and that it presents a linear discussion, moving logically from one part to the next. There are expectations regarding the style of writing: a seemingly 'objective' narrative written in the third person is the norm, interspersed with textual evidence from other such studies, possibly in the form of quotations in the case of a literary study. When writing a PhD thesis it is presumed that one will adhere to these conventions but I decided to embark on a rather different venture by writing it in the form of a series of fictitious letters, using two imaginary correspondences as the framework. Its aim was to explore the traditional framework of a PhD thesis, to expose the limitations of its structure and to offer commentary on the process of writing.

The aim of this letter is to illustrate that 'epistolary criticism' – literary criticism in letter form – can prove to be an exciting experiment for the critic and reader alike. More specifically, it will lead you through the rationale of my somewhat unconventional PhD thesis on the work of Welsh poet, Menna Elfyn (see Marks, 2011).

I must admit it is more by chance than intention that I came across epistolary criticism since I would never have imagined at the outset that I would spend my years as a PhD student writing fictitious letters. My initial aim was to research the relationship between feminism and Welsh language poetry but my frustration with the process of categorizing texts soon highlighted the complex nature of the relationship between author, text and reader in the process of interpreting. I found myself in quite a predicament wondering whether it was a good idea to categorize women as 'feminist' poets. Morever I was uneasy with regards to how a text could be classified as a 'feminist' text, since texts can be read in several ways.

On hearing feminist critic Toril Moi's lecture 'I am not a woman writer' (Moi, 2008) where she discussed the term 'woman writer' and asked a very provocative question – 'Is it always in the feminist interest to read women writers as *women* writers?' – I started considering my own application of the term in the context of Welsh literature particularly in relation to poetry. On reading Hilary Llewellyn-Williams's poem 'The Woman Poet' (Gramich and Brennan, 2003: 314–5, I started to wonder whether such a character actually existed, since couldn't see also be defined by other characteristics? I also wondered whether it was a good idea to identify poetry composed by women as 'women's poetry' since there are many preconceptions regarding this, for instance that they are obsessed with writing about the body, or that their writing is immersed in emotion or that it is as Jane Dowson puts it 'hysterical, melancholy, solipsistic and technically inferior' (Dowson, 1999: 13).

The result of my dissatisfaction with gender as an essence was to doubt the significance of all types of essentialist readings as I found them insufficient and incomprehensive of my experience as a reader. Despite being revelatory to a certain degree, reading texts as the products of a particular social class, ethnicity, gender or as the reflection of a historical period or political mood/trend, only provides a limited reading. Moreover, fencing authors and works into neat pens does not truly encapsulate the real experiences of a reader. Schweickart and Flynn raise a similar matter in their volume *Reading Sites: Social Difference and Reader Response* where they emphasize the need to move away from essentialist readings of works written by women rather than 'homogenize all differences into the master category of gender' (Schweickart and Flynn, 2004: 18). Their proposition is 'to think not of one general other but of particular others, differentiated, among other things, by race, ethnicity, and class'. Bearing this in mind I decided to concentrate specifically on the work of one woman writer in order to consider the significance of gender and its interaction with other factors.

Menna Elfyn

I chose to concentrate on the poetry of contemporary poet Menna Elfyn (1951–). Her list of publications is impressive and to date includes eight volumes of poetry in Welsh as well as five bilingual English/Welsh volumes: *Eucalyptus* (1995), *Cell Angel* (1996), *Cusan Dyn Dall/Blind Man's Kiss* (2001), *Perfect Blemish/Perffaith Nam* (2007) and *Murmur* (2012). On the publication of her first bilingual volume, Elfyn was described by Anthony Conran as 'the first Welsh poet in fifteen hundred years to make a serious attempt to have her work known outside Wales' (Conran cited in Elfyn, 1995: xi), and she is indeed the most translated of all Welsh language poets. Elfyn is often described by the labels 'feminist, nationalist and pacifist' since her early writing is very politically engaged. Several of these poems are polemical in tone or take issue with political matters such as the battle to ensure the future of the Welsh language during the 1970s and 1980s, the women's stand for peace at Greenham, and the rights of all kinds of minority groups who fight against injustice. She admits in her essay 'Writing is a Bird in Hand' that when she started out 'as a poet and protester, my aim was not only to change the status of the language but to change society as well' (Elfyn, 1994: 282). One of my main reasons for choosing Menna Elfyn was that she is labelled 'Wales's best known feminist poet' (Hunter, 1998: 143) and much emphasis has been placed on the way in which she gives voice to the experiences of women in her work (see Gramich, 2007; Thomas, 1999). My aim was to challenge this categorization, and show, or suggest at least, that other factors apart from gender should be taken into account when reading her work since her poetry is multifaceted and can be read in several ways.

I was also keen to explore the concept of literary value, since Menna Elfyn's poems were rejected by the editors of the Welsh anthology, *Blodeugerdd o Farddoniaeth Gymraeg yr Ugeinfed Ganrif,* on the grounds that they weren't considered to be worthy or 'teilwng' (Llwyd, 1988: 12–3). My aim was to question this notion of 'worthiness' and suggest that a literary text has no intrinsic value since the process of evaluating a text is constantly repeated and reassessed as one reads. Barbara Hernstein Smith notes that:

> ... a work's value [is] seen not as something already fixed in it and indicated by particular critical judgements but, rather, as numerous different effects continuously produced and sustained by those very evaluative activities and practices themselves. (Smith, 1990: 181)

I was keen to create a thesis that would illustrate the complexities of the process of giving meaning to a text.

On finalizing a topic, the problem that then faced me was the medium of discussion. How could I write a thesis that would allow me to pull together several different strands of discussion and at the same time depict the process of reading? Furthermore, how could I write a thesis that would satisfy the creative writer in me?

A source of inspiration was a project that was being carried out in America at the time entitled *Letters to Poets: Conversation about Poetics, Politics and Community.* The book has since been published and comprises of correspondences between poets over a period of twelve months. In their letters the poets mainly discuss matters pertaining to poetry including the role of politics, gender, race and ethnicity in literary works as well as discussions on the processes of reading and writing. In the words of the editors: 'we hope that these letters will spark discussion and offer insight into some of the ongoing urgent conversations in contemporary poetry' (Lomax and Firestone, 2006).

It certainly sparked an interest in me, and the notion of writing a personal response to a literary text in the form of a letter appeared extremely appealing. It seemed that the personal nature of the letter form would allow me to explore the process of my reading therefore I started experimenting with the genre to find out whether or not this was the case. My initial idea was to write a fictitious letter to the poet Menna Elfyn discussing her work, so I chose a poem and wondered what I would discuss with the poet if I were to send her a letter. The genre was full of potential since it allowed me to present a personal reading of the text in a creative and somewhat unconventional way.

It's a method that demands a leap of the imagination on behalf of the author and reader alike since the concept of writing letters to a poet who's alive but who'll never actually receive them seems bizarre to say the least. But, as I wrote more letters of this kind I realized that writing a PhD thesis in the form of a series of letters allowed me the freedom to go in directions that a more conventional essay form doesn't allow.

First, it provides the opportunity to place a reading in a personal and specific context in terms of time and place. This enables me to be fairly honest while reading and to express uncertainty with regards to a text's meaning. The fact that each reading is anchored in a specific time period allows me to show that research is a process that happens and develops over time rather than being a timeless finished process. It also gives me as a reader a valuable opportunity to interpret a poem in more than one way, and allows me to revisit a poem in a later letter and discover in it something different to what had initially read. The creative nature of this literary form allows me to be quite playful when it comes to interpreting and permits me to experiment with the discourse usually expected of literary criticism. Finally, it admits openly what is true of every form of criticism – even the strictest form of structuralism – that, ultimately, it is selective and subjective.

I must admit that I had my doubts at times during the project and wondered whether a thesis written in the form of a fictitious correspondence would actually work and whether the letter form could be sustained throughout the entire project. I therefore turned to look more closely at correspondences to study the use of this genre.

The letter form has been both a popular and useful form over the years for discussing matters such as literature and philosophy and correspondences between authors often provide an illuminating response to the literary atmosphere of their time. A correspondence that particularly fascinated me is the one shared by Welsh writers R. S. Thomas and Raymond Garlick (Walford Davies, 2009) where they discuss, among other things, their responses to one another's poems and their perceptions of the literary scene. On reading this volume it confirmed what I had previously thought: the letter form provides the writer with a way of expressing one's personal response to a text. Also, since the letters were mostly written in the latter half of the twentieth century they provide a valuable insight into the happenings of the Anglo-Welsh literary scene of the time. It soon struck me that my own correspondence needn't necessarily be restricted to readings of poems but that they could be used for example to illustrate the significance of literary events.

This correspondence inspired, albeit indirectly, a letter discussing a public poetry reading by Menna Elfyn at the Hay Festival – a festival which, despite being held within the Welsh border is generally not as well attended by Welsh-language speakers as what is considered the main Welsh literary festival of the year: the Welsh National Eisteddfod. The letter form allowed me to explore the context of the reception of the Elfyn's poems at this event and to discuss the relationship between performativity and poetry. The fact that letters are always grounded in a specific time and place allowed me to discuss my expectations regarding performing poetry before this particular event, and to follow it up with a letter recounting the experience, and admitting that some of my preconceptions were proved wrong. Epistolary criticism allows me to change my mind and to argue against what has been stated previously at a later date.

Reading correspondences that are more fictional in nature, such as Lisa Williams's *Letters to Virginia Woolf*, also proved to be quite an inspiration. In the course of the volume Williams presents an imaginary correspondence with the celebrated author and discusses her own experiences of life in post 9/11 New York, in the light of reading Woolf's work. It was interesting to see how the correspondence provides Williams with the means of making a connection with the celebrated author's work and to present her reading in the form of a fictional literary response. It was also useful to see how a 'narrative' could be sustained throughout by presenting only one side of the imagined correspondence.

In a similar way, Fay Weldon's *Letters to Alice on first reading Jane Austen* explores the potential of the letter for discussing literary works, where 'Aunt Fay', writes letters to her niece Alice in order to persuade her to read the Austen's work. The letters provide Weldon with a means of discussing Austen's novels in a creative and often humorous way. The notion of an instructional correspondence, which may be considered in the same vein as that of R. M. Rilke's *Letters to a Young Poet,* grabbed my interest and it seemed that it could be incorporated into my project.

My original intention was to write a series of letters to Menna Elfyn but I soon found that composing a letter to the poet herself, and writing in the second person had its limitations. Stylistically, I feared that at times it was monotonous, and it didn't quite sound convincing that I was constantly addressing the poet saying 'in your poem you discuss ... '. Critically, there was no way of putting her work into context for the empirical reader of my essay, that being the examiner. Due to the overwhelming urge of wanting to adhere to convention and write about the poetry in the third person I introduced another correspondent to the project. It took some time to envisage the fictional character since I was aware that many characteristics of his/her identity would determine or at least influence the nature of his/her reading of texts, and hence would steer the project in a specific direction. There were many questions to consider: should the character be male or female? How old should he or she be? To what culture should he or she belong and what should be the language of our correspondence? Even the character's name posed a dilemma.

Finally it was decided that she should be a first year university student who wanted to learn more about the poetry of Menna Elfyn. Perhaps she might best be described as someone who, unintentionally, resembles a depiction of a younger 'version' of myself. Portrayed as one who is studying Welsh at University, she is keen to develop new ways of reading texts. Her name is Martha and she was christened thus in order to echo eminent Welsh writer, William Williams Pantycelyn's 'Llythyr Martha Philopur at y Parchedig Philo Evangelius ei Hathro' (1762) and 'Atteb Philo-Evangelius i Martha Philopur' (1763). Pantycelyn's letters are essentially instructional texts presented in the form of a fictitious correspondence in which a young girl writes to her teacher, Philo-Evangelius, asking for guidance in reading the Bible. In the same way that Pantycelyn's Martha is a naive reader who wishes to know whether her reading is 'correct', my Martha asks questions about the text that she is reading: the work of Menna Elfyn. Some letters contextualize the poetry for instance, whereas others suggest readings of poems through the lens of a certain theoretical school and attempt to challenge Martha's preconceptions regarding the process of reading.

The introduction of Martha proved to be a useful literary device – her character provides another thread to the weave of the narrative, as it were, but she also serves a valuable purpose in providing a critical counterpoint. The letters are set in a framework of three years in order that her three undergraduate years run alongside my doctoral research. As our correspondence develops she is portrayed as one who has gained confidence in critical reading, and therefore can challenge many of the arguments that I put forward in my letters to her. This enabled me to illustrate two sides of an argument in a dialogic way; something that might not be so easily done in a conventional academic essay where emphasis is placed on developing *a thesis* rather than *theses*.

By including the letters to Martha alongside the letters to Menna, it allows me to depict at least two dimensions of the reader in me. On the one hand, in letters to Martha I'm fairly confident in my interpretation since our imagined relationship is fairly instructive on my part. The letters to Menna on the other hand expose a more questioning reader – one who isn't sure how to read the work, and who expresses the perplexity that is felt when trying to get to grips with some of the more difficult poems. The two sets of correspondences combined therefore allow me to practise separately two voices that are often entwined in critical discourse – a narrative voice and an inquisitive voice.

Two 'voices' proved to be better than one, but I decided to experiment further with another voice – a typically 'academic' one – and therefore included two conventional chapters and a conference paper in the correspondence in order to draw attention to their limitations. In the narrative this is framed by suggesting that I'm writing a PhD thesis and that I'm sending the chapters to Martha so that she can read them along with a letter discussing the shortcomings of the chapters and the difficulties that arose when writing. This provided me with an invaluable opportunity to critique my own chapters, and to draw attention to the difficulties that arose in the process of writing them.

In essence, what is illustrated in the work is the *mise en abyme* concept. In the same way that Shakespeare's *Hamlet* contains a play within a play, and Diego Velázquez's famous painting *Las Meninas* depicts the process of painting in the painting itself, my own work consists of an 'essay' within an 'essay'. By combining the correspondence and the more conventional academic chapters, it allows for a polyphonic kind of criticism where several voices or discourses can co-exist, where one genre seen next to another is revelatory in the sense that it draws attention to the characteristics of both genres involved.

Challenging academic conventions

Anne Bower in her book *Epistolary Responses: The Letter in 20th-Century American Fiction and Criticism* emphasizes the usefulness of the letter form for critical writing. Indeed, she goes as far as to suggest that the freedom provided by the form could prove to be a breath of fresh air within the academic institution and academic writing:

> In the same way that the letter form provides epistolary characters with a mode of responding to others, with the chance to rewrite themselves and others, criticism in letter form helps us to rewrite our concepts of academic discourse, perhaps even our concepts of the academic institution. (Bower, 1997: 8)

She suggests that such a form of criticism provides a valuable opportunity to make an unusual connection between the author of a text and its reader, which could lead to a reassessment of this important relationship:

> At one or more levels – emotional, psychological, political, intellectual – 'lettered' criticism holds the potential to change the writer, the reader, the critical act, and the relationships among them. (Bower, 1997: 181)

Certainly, in the course of my project I've found that the letter form allows me to both depict and analyse the constantly changing nature of the relationship between the author, the text, and the reader.

By writing letters I can draw attention to the process of reading and illustrate that there isn't just one way of reading a text. The fact that every letter is grounded in a particular time and place, allows me to revisit some of Menna Elfyn's poems in more than one letter in order to illustrate that, as Susan Noakes suggests in her volume *Timely Reading*: 'there is not just one way to read, [...] reading (whether one recognizes it or not) is always a process of investigating and making choices' (Noakes, 1988: 230). Emphasis is placed on the choices that are made in the light of new information acquired since a previous reading. This method therefore allows me to illustrate the unstable nature of a text's meaning, and that there isn't such a thing as a 'final reading'.

The personal nature of the work allows me to depict how a reading of Menna Elfyn's texts are conditioned by extra textual discourses. Factors, such as previous readings, prejudices, the reader's political ideas, other people's opinions, and more importantly the reading community to which the reader belongs, influence the manner in which texts are read. Attention is given to these factors in the course of the correspondence.

There is room for a certain degree of honesty in the work in the sense that it is possible to depict and recount the steps of a reader's reaction to a text. For instance, some letters try to capture the enjoyment derived from reading Elfyn's work but since some poems can be quite complex and unclear at times, it is possible to use the personal nature of the letter form to express the difficulty that I came across in certain poems when attempting to define particular words and give meaning to phrases. To an extent, there is a degree of dishonesty too since the work itself is just as much of an illusion and a 'creation' as a PhD thesis. However, a typical academic essay would not so readily allow one to admit one's shortcomings. It is possible to show in the letters how someone, at times, can misread lines of works but rather than depicting this as a 'failure' of understanding I hope to show that it's part of the process of reading. After all, as Karin Littau states, 'To read [...] according to the logic of deconstruction is always to risk misunderstanding and hence potentially misreading. To deconstruction, misreading is not a failure of correct understanding since the notion of a correct reading is a fallacy' (Littau, 2006: 106).

The correspondence also provides a way of drawing attention to the process of composing literary criticism since the project, in its entirety, attempts to criticize the critical process. Authors of literary criticism usually arrange their ideas into neat chapters – usually thematically or chronologically – but my project attempts to challenge this convention by being creative with the criticism. The division of work into chapters suggests that an author has come to a final conclusion about a text and that the conclusion falls neatly into categories and sub-categories. I wish to suggest that this is an artificial convention to all extents and purposes and that it does not, in any way, reflect the process of reading. After all, the process of interpreting a text is not a neat, tidy one since a reader does not often explore the corpus of a bard's work thematically or in chronological order.

The reception of the work – A 'contribution' v. conservatism

The decision to write the thesis through the medium of the Welsh language also had its implications. Since I was enrolled as a PhD student in the Department of Welsh at Aberystwyth it seemed logical that I should write in Welsh because that is the main language of instruction at the department, and it is my maternal language. The decision was also driven by a desire to contribute to the developing field of Welsh literary criticism and to engage in dialogue with other practitioners whose work I greatly respect. However, it also meant that I had to deal with the implications of writing within a minority language culture where there is a constant struggle between tradition and innovation. The interaction of both forces in a field that might be considered quite conservative in nature creates an interesting dynamic, yet from the perspective of a young researcher venturing to publish a fictional correspondence it can cause some trepidation. Interestingly, in the creative non-fiction conference from which this chapter (or rather, letter) is derived, one participant asked whether my work would be readily accepted by those in Welsh academia since it would be seen as a contribution to a relatively small, yet growing field. In actual fact, so far it is in conferences in Wales that I have had to most justify the academic integrity of my project.

The volume is presently on its way to press (see Marks, 2013), and like all texts, it will be at the mercy of potential readers and their individual processes of reading. There is a slight feeling of uneasiness on my part with regards to its reception, but as Salman Rushdie once said of the process of sending a text out into the unkown – 'you've done what you can and you've set it afloat. Now it's up to it to sink or swim ... ' (Fenton, 1991). I'll let you know how it goes.

Well, I hope that I've managed to persuade you that epistolary criticism offers numerous possibilities to the author and reader alike. Jacques Derrida praised the possibilities of the letter form and mentions in 'Envois' that it's not a *genre* that should be pushed to one side and forgotten, but that it's a key to understand more about literature: 'La lettre, l'êpitre, qui n'est pas un genre mais tous les genres, la littérature même' (Derrida, 1980: 54).

Thank you for reading.

Yours sincerely,

Rhiannon Marks

Acknowledgements

Since writing this article, the PhD thesis on which this study is based has been published (see Marks, 2013).

References

Bower, A. (1997) *Epistolary Responses*. Tuscaloosa: The University of Alabama Press.

Conran, A. (1999) 'preface' to M. Elfyn, *Eucalyptus*, Llandysul: Gwasg Gomer.

Derrida, J. (1980) *La Carte Postale*. Flammarion.

Dowson, J. (1999) 'Older Sisters are Very Sobering Things': Contemporary Women Poets and the Female Affiliation Complex', *Feminist Review* 62: 6–20.

Elfyn, M. (1994) 'Writing as a bird in hand', in J. Aaron, T. Rees, S. Betts and M. Vincentelli, *Our Sisters' Land: The Changing Identities of Women in Wales*, pp. 280–6. Cardiff: University of Wales Press.

Fenton, J. (1991) 'Keeping up with Salman Rushdie', *The New York Review of Books* 38, accessed March 2009, http://www.nybooks.com/articles/archives/1991/mar/28/keeping-up-with-salman-rushdie/

Gramich, K. (2007) *Twentieth-Century Women's Writing in Wales*. Cardiff: University of Wales Press.

Gramich, K. and Brennan, C. (2003) *Welsh Women's Poetry 1460–2001*. Dinas Powys: Gwasg Honno.

Hunter, T. G. (1998) 'Contemporary Welsh Poetry: 1969–1996', in Dafydd Johnston (ed.) *A Guide to Welsh Literature c.1900–1996*, pp. 117–58. Cardiff: University of Wales Press.

Littau, K. (2006) *Theories of Reading*. Cambridge: Polity Press.

Llwyd, A. (1988) 'Golygyddol', *Barddas* 135–7(1): 12–5, Gorffennaf/Awst/Medi.

Lomax, D. T. and Firestone, J, (2006) 'Editor's note', *Jacket Magazine* 31, accessed February 2008, http://jacketmagazine.com/31/lett-intro.html

Marks, R. (2011) '"Pe Gallwn, Mi Luniwn Lythyr": ymdriniaeth feirniadol â gwaith Menna Elfyn trwy ohebiaeth ffuglenol' (unpublished PhD thesis, the University of Aberystwyth).

Marks, R. (2013) *'Pe Gallwn, Mi Luniwn Lythyr': golwg ar waith Menna Elfyn*. Caerdydd: Gwasg Prifysgol Cymru.

Moi, T. (2008) '"I am not a woman writer": About women, literature and feminist theory today', *Feminist Theory* 9: 259–71.

Noakes, S. (1988) *Timely Reading: Between Exegesis and Interpretation.* London: Cornell University Press.
Schweickart, P. P. and Flynn, E. A. (2004) *Reading Sites: Social Difference and Reader Response.* New York: Modern Language Association of America.
Smith, B. H. (1990) *Critical Terms for Literary Study*. London: Chicago Press.
Thomas, M. W. (1999) 'The place of gender in the poetry of Gillian Clarke and Menna Elfyn', *Corresponding Cultures: the two literatures of Wales,* pp. 186–213. Cardiff: University of Wales Press.
Walford Davies, J. (2009) *R. S. Thomas: Letters to Raymond Garlick, 1959–1999*. Llandysul: Gomer Press.

An Introduction to 'Schizoanalysis'
The Development of a Musical Approach to Criticism

Jo Collinson Scott

Introductory Questions: Conceptual Music

As an undergraduate student many years ago, I was once asked to write an analysis of a piece of music by a modern 12-tone composer. Although I would normally start the process of analysing a piece by first listening to it whilst looking at the score, in this instance I began my research by doing extensive reading about the piece and looking at written analyses. In the course of reading I was quite overwhelmed by the beauty of the ideas that were being described as being the basis for the piece. There was the exploration of exquisite crystalline forms and how they could be made musical; there were deft and inspirational mathematical manoeuvres. The piece was built from a number of very beautiful and original ideas that moved me. I read as much as I could about the piece, becoming increasingly excited to hear the results of such stunning conceptual manipulations. When I finally put my headphones on and listened however, I was disappointed. The aesthetic and theoretical appreciation I had for the ideas that created the music, and thus my *idea of* the music, was much greater than the effect of the resulting sounds. So much greater in fact, that I wished I had been left only with the ideas and not with the sound. In the moment of wishing to deny the aural outworking of the piece, I began to ask myself about the nature of the thing I had been previously appreciating. If it was not the *sound* of the piece that I was engaging with, was it even music I was enjoying? If not – if it was something else – then what was this thing? My response to it certainly seemed more akin to an aesthetic enjoyment than a purely intellectual appreciation. Was it the skill of the analyst I was appreciating; the artistry of analysis? Or some kind of 'art' of the compositional process? Or was I creating my own internal composition in my mind in response to these ideas, and it was this mental music that I was responding to? Further, I began to wonder if anyone else had felt this way, indeed, if anyone else in composing a piece had decided to simply stop once the idea of the music had been formulated, and left it at that, believing the result to be a kind of music in itself.

On beginning to research these questions I discovered a handful of works of what could be called 'Conceptual music' that emerged mainly from musicians at work within the American Conceptual art movement in the 1950s and 1960s. They were the best examples I could find of works that started out from the point of view of privileging composers' *ideas of music* (be that ontological, epistemological, speculative philosophical, aesthetic idealist, cognitive, etc.) over the resultant sound. Indeed, some of the questions I posed that day in the music library, with my headphones discarded around my neck (such as, *what if there were no sound, just ideas about sound – would that still be music?*) were exactly the types of questions that Conceptual music sought to pose through its very form (or lack of form).

Peter Goldie and Elisabeth Schellekens, in their important philosophical exploration, *Who's Afraid of Conceptual Art*, have ventured a useful way of defining what underpins all the extremely varied types of artistic output that seem to constitute the movement. This method can also be applied to an understanding of what constitutes a work of Conceptual music. They explain Conceptual works as 'enacted thought experiments' (Goldie and Schellekens, 2010: 9). This means that the provocative nature of the form (or lack of form) and the linguistic content of these works acts as a proposed idea and serves to help uncover the nature of commonly held, but perhaps unexamined, ideas about music.[1] They then seek to test these ideas to destruction – exploring the outer reaches of any definition or boundary idea. Conceptual artworks and pieces of Conceptual music test ideas that, in their testing, present a challenge to philosophical understandings of the terms 'art' and 'music'. By their very nature they represent ontological and epistemological questions for the art/music world and the public. Thus, these Conceptual works function like thought experiments in philosophy but are enacted as objects.[2]

Musical works that can be counted as Conceptual works that are enacted thought experiments include John Cage's *4'33"*, which seeks to pose questions such as, *if we were to listen to the sounds the audience makes during a performance as if those sounds were the musical performance, would they become music?* La Monte Young's *Composition # 5, 1960* serves to ask the listener, *what if the sound of a piece were too quiet to hear, would it still be music?* And George Brecht's collection of word scores, *Water Yam*, tests the hypothesis, among others, that the essential aspects of musical performance immediately preceding or following the actual production of sound constitute music themselves.

It seemed then, upon discovery of these pieces, that some of the questions I had been asking were addressed by the existence of these works of Conceptual music. However, it also seemed that my examination of these pieces in the context of musicology or music criticism unleashed questions much larger than the original foundational question. First, in attempting to study these works, I encountered the obvious problem that works without any 'sound' to speak of present to the standard tools of music analysis. Any attempt at a formalist analysis of a work of music when that work does not consist of any physical sound properties, or even the definitive representation of those sound properties in a score, is extremely difficult. There simply isn't any recognizable *form* to analyse. Even more difficult is analysing or criticizing a work that has been specifically formulated and presented in order to thwart that purpose. Furthermore, these musical works are no longer separated from criticism by a divide between 'language' and 'sound'. In many of these works, the music takes the form of written language, or of concepts (which are often represented as lingual entities). This means that the easy division between 'music' and 'words about music' is being challenged and dismantled. It was here – in the arena of challenges to formalist approaches to music criticism – where another strand of my journey towards development of a form of creative non-fiction was emerging.

Opening up the Act of Criticism: New Musicology and Conceptual Music

In the last thirty years or so, certain sectors of the field of musicology have been moving away from formalist approaches to analysis and have developed a range of new forms of criticism that are less dependent on formal elements of the music. This includes the output of 'new musicologists', whose work challenges the longstanding idea that music is a text that is not affected by and does not affect politics, gender issues, culture, human emotions, reception, context, etc.[3] For example, many of those who were writing about music in the 1980s and 1990s (particularly feminist musicologists, and those in the field of queer studies) felt that what was missing from their academic work was a sense of their own relation to the music: their bodily interactions with it, their emotions as a listener, their own creativity. The effect of the pioneering work of the new musicologists in this regard has therefore served within the field to allow the 'extra-musical' to be brought into discussions of music in terms of its meaning, its function, its effect, its importance, and its worth.[4]

Returning to the new possibilities opened up to me as a critic by the peculiar anti-formal nature of Conceptual music, my interest in emerging forms of musicology wasn't related to greater freedom to express my emotional or visceral reactions to music in an academic context, where previously this was considered too subjective. Nor was it related to the range of 'other' texts that could now be brought to bear on analysis of music. Instead, my enthusiasm about the widening of forms of academic music criticism came from a glimpse of the potential for creativity within the act of criticism itself. My question had now become whether as a critic I could create a work of art, or piece of music, with my critical writing.

Previously – within a long history of academic musicological focus on objectivity, formalism, scientific methodologies, quantifiable results, etc. – my experience was that any creativity inherent in the act of writing about music was relegated to secondary status, if acknowledged at all. However, through close explorations of the work of Conceptual musicians and new musicologists it has become clear that there is a place where my creative response to music can be explored within an academic context. This is the place where Conceptual music and music criticism cross over.

Osborne writes that what he calls 'strong' conceptualism, 'took the ultimate form of the attempt to efface the categorical difference between art and criticism in the polemical presentation of critical discourse as itself art, in the journal *Art-Language*, for example' (Osborne, 1999: 59). Within this challenge, posed by the breaking down of the barrier between the subject and object of criticism in art, there is the glimpse of an exciting opportunity with relation to music too – for music criticism to become musical.

It was clear at this point in my investigations that I needed a model for such work from the theoretical field. Where Conceptual music questioned the boundaries of music from within the genre of music itself, I required examples of works that might serve to question the boundaries of criticism from within criticism itself. And I found one such potential model in Gregory Ulmer's conception of *Applied Grammatology*.

In his book *Applied Grammatology: Post(e)-Pedagogy from Jacques Derrida to Joseph Beuys*, Ulmer points out that Derrida's highly influential practice of deconstruction has been the focus for those who have driven through the massive changes in most humanities subjects (including musicology) in terms of opening up texts to that which previously would have seen as lying 'outside' them. However, Ulmer demonstrates that there is a clear difference in the way that Derrida treats philosophical works (which he deconstructs) and the way that he treats artistic or literary works. Ulmer suggests that he doesn't deconstruct the works he considers, but *mimes* them instead. Ulmer describes how Derrida treats these works as, 'models or tutors to be imitated, as generative forms for the production of another text' (Ulmer, 1992: xi). So whereas deconstruction is a mode of analysis, 'Writing' or 'Grammatology' is a mode of composition. Ulmer describes his understanding of the application of grammatology (which he proposes as a practice called 'post-criticism') as follows:

> As if following Wittgenstein's admonition that 'the meaning is the use', Derrida enacts or performs (mimes) the compositional structuration of the referent, resulting in another text of the same 'kind' [...] Post-Criticism, then, functions with an 'epistemology' of performance – knowing as making, producing, doing, acting [...] Thus post-criticism writes 'on' its object [...] (Ulmer, 1998: 107).

Derrida's example of an alternative approach to art or music criticism involves the creation of a text that acts in the same way as the text in question, with the same materials, thus to mime its action.

It seems that Conceptual music as outlined here – a critique of music presented *as* music – should be an appropriate place to begin an exploration into the applicability and efficacy of such a grammatological approach to music. As in the case of Conceptual music, Derrida's grammatological work serves to elucidate its subject, as well as questioning what it means to philosophise, or elucidate. Crucially, this means that if its subject were to be music, then at the same time as it questioned music, it would also embody music: it would *be* music.

My thesis then, is that Conceptual music can be used as a model for enacting an alternative or experimental form of music criticism, which in this instance I have called 'schizoanalysis'. This is the process of conducting something akin to enacted thought experiments. Thus schizoanalytical texts are critical texts that do philosophical work (they propose a hypothesis, and they explore that hypothesis), but they are also 'enacted', i.e. they are creative, artistic works. The specific thought experiment that is being enacted in my texts is an exploration of the hypothesis that music criticism can be a form of music. This is both the sense in which schizoanalysis is a reflection of the means by which Conceptual music does its work, and the way in which it poses a question concerning new forms of music criticism.

The Relationship of Schizophrenia to Conceptual Music and Creative Criticism

As an undergraduate student of music and psychology, for a time I had the misfortune of a clash of lectures. My second year music class, *Aspects of Modernity*, finished roughly ten minutes into my hour-long *Abnormal Psychology* lecture – a pattern that was repeated on a weekly basis and left me consistently arriving conspicuous and red-in-the-face, one sixth less well-prepared than the rest of my psychology peers. On the face of it this would seem to be nothing more notable than a disadvantageous scheduling anomaly, however from the very first week I was aware of something extremely interesting emerging.

The weekly correlation threw up quite obvious parallels, deeper and deeper similarities, greater and greater understanding between schizophrenic symptoms and some of the defining features of modernist movements in music. On investigating this further I came upon the work of clinical psychologist Louis Sass.

In his book *Madness and Modernism*, Louis Sass has formulated a phenomenological understanding of schizophrenia that uses the parallel characteristics of certain modern philosophies, literatures and artistic practices as an analogy, or, in his words, an enlightening 'affinity', in order to attempt to understand and engage with the lived experience of schizophrenia (Sass, 1992: 9). He points out endless and varied ways in which the diverse and often radically alien features of modernism in philosophy, literature and the arts are remarkably similar to the symptoms or manifestations of schizophrenic experience. In following through Sass's conception of the progress of schizophrenia – its phenomenological basis and its symptomatology – I was aware of more and more areas where schizophrenic thought patterns, use of language, forms of reasoning, and inner experiences, served to highlight the musicality of language. Over time, this began to suggest to me that these phenomena might demonstrate the potential means of the creation of forms of critical practice that were musical. These experimental forms I have called 'schizoanalyses'.

Notes Regarding the use of Terms 'Schizophrenia' and 'Schizoanalysis'

Before I continue on to describe how I propose that schizophrenic thinking might be used in the formation of a creative criticism that 'mimes' musical works (a schizoanalysis), I do need to clarify my use of the term 'schizophrenia'. The aim of this project is in no way to pathologize artists and musicians of the modern or post-modern era. I do not wish to draw any kind of causal link between schizophrenia and the arts. Furthermore, the use of the term should in no way be looked upon as either a trivialization or a glorification of the condition.

Angela Woods, in her examination of the use of schizophrenia as a topoi in modern cultural discourse, has found it helpful to define two types of approach to schizophrenia – clinical and cultural (Woods, 2011). She defines 'clinical theory' as, 'work that aims to achieve a clinically meaningful outcome', and is achieved through analysis of the patient. Clinical theory would include the medical-model of schizophrenia. On the other hand, 'cultural theories' of schizophrenia seek insight into aspects of twentieth-century culture using the understanding that schizophrenia in all its forms can give them (for example Fredric Jameson's [1984/2000] use of the term in *Postmodernism, Or the Cultural Logic of Late Capitalism*). These cultural theories are a result of the important work of Lacan in the psychoanalysis of schizophrenia, where schizophrenia began to be described in terms of the breakdown of the signifying chain in language. His work also contrasted the autonomous, paranoid, modern self with a schizophrenic, hyper-reflexive, problematized and open self. This meant schizophrenia became a key topoi in exploring the nature of postmodern culture.

Sass's phenomenological approach, however, can be seen as an unusual hybrid of cultural and clinical understandings of schizophrenia. One the one hand, Sass uses comparison to cultural phenomena in order to develop his understanding of schizophrenic symptoms. On the other hand, he sticks solely to verifiable clinical case studies of schizophrenic experience, working in the clinical field himself with schizophrenic patients. The reason for the importance of this approach is that purely cultural theories of schizophrenia such as Jameson's, for example, can easily fall foul of what Glass calls a terrible 'error', in 'the postmodernist interpretation of what multiplicity of self *means*' (Glass, 1993: 257, emphasis in original). In separating off the morbid aspects of schizophrenia, these theories tend to reach a point of valorizing or celebrating schizophrenic experience as joyous or freeing. Angela Woods takes issue with this strategy in Jameson's *Postmodernism*, where she says his use of a clinical example rather than, 'say, an artistic portrayal of "unreality", works against Jameson's clinical agnosticism" (Woods, 2011: 200). This is a fundamental misinterpretation of the experience of schizophrenia, according to many researchers who work day to day in clinical settings with people suffering under the clinical diagnosis 'schizophrenia'. Elsewhere, James Glass reminds theorists that, 'the evaluation of theories of power, domination and patriarchy is important and useful, but if it utilises schizophrenia as a model for the "ideal" deconstructed identity [... it] is irresponsible and insensitive to the human costs of this illness' (Glass, 1995: 15).

Before continuing, I should also clarify my use of the term 'schizoanalysis'. This must be distinguished from Deleuze and Guattari's specific use of that same term, and is related only in general terms to their practice of schizoanalysis (Deleuze and Guattari, 2004a,b). I feel able to use the same term because their endeavour was born from the same need – the need for a specific model with which to analyse a subject. And the model of schizophrenia was appropriate to the embodiment of certain important aspects of both their subject and my own. However, the subjects of my analyses are very different to those of Deleuze and Guattari (works of Conceptual music as opposed to Marxist flows of capital and Freudian flows of desire in Capitalism), and therefore, the specific means of those analyses are different. The clinical methodology I have chosen through which to understand schizophrenic experience is different to theirs (Sass's phenomenology as opposed to Guattari's psychoanalysis; Sass's unique mix of the clinical and the cultural, as opposed to Deleuze and Guattari's focus on cultural analysis), and the aspects of schizophrenic experience on which I have chosen to focus are therefore very different, as are the resulting forms of these analyses.[5] I should also emphasize that 'schizoanalysis' is not an existing term within musicology. The use of applied grammatology to analyse music, or the use of other creative or quasi-musical methods to respond to works of music has not, as far as I am aware, not been attempted so far in academic literature.

Parallels between Key Schizophrenic Symptoms and Features of Conceptual Music

Perhaps the main way in which Conceptual music can be related to schizophrenia is through the concept of hyper-reflexivity. Researchers and theorists of the Ipseity-Hyperreflexivity model of schizophrenia (derived from Sass's observations on schizophrenia and modernism in the arts) have shown that many schizophrenic symptoms can be caused by over-reflection on the nature of the self. As laid out by Sass and Parnas in 2011, the 'IHM' view suggests that, 'instability of pre-reflexive self-awareness is a core, generative feature of schizophrenia' (Sass, 2011: 7). This means that as perceptions of the world become altered for the schizophrenic in early symptomatic experience, attention is naturally turned to the originator of means of perception (the 'self'), which then becomes increasingly elusive under scrutiny. One can only take so many steps back from experience in order to get perspective on its nature before the unself-conscious embodiment of that experience – a sense of 'self' – seems very far away. Hyper-reflexivity can also be shown to be absolutely key to the workings of Conceptual art and Conceptual music, which as we have seen, are defined and created by a continual and intensive reflection on the nature of 'art' or 'music'. Indeed, Adrian Piper has described the work of Sol LeWitt and first-generation conceptualists as restoring, 'distanced self-awareness as a central value of artistic production' in their art (Piper, 1993/2000: 548). In the introduction to his textbook, *Conceptual Art*, Tony Godfrey again makes explicit the key relationship between a schizophrenic-type hyper-reflection on the self and the work of the Conceptual artist as an enacted thought experiment:

> If a work of Conceptual art begins with the question 'What is art?' rather than a particular style or medium, one could argue that it is

> completed by the proposition, 'This could be art': 'this' being presented as object, image, performance or idea revealed in some other way. Conceptual art is therefore 'reflexive': the object refers back to the subject, as in the phrase 'I am thinking about how I think.' It represents a state of continual self-critique. (Godfrey, 1998: 12)

The nature of music criticism is also drawn into this reflexivity, bound as it is to definitions of both music and criticism that separate these ideas conceptually from other practices. This becomes particularly apparent when the means of Conceptual music's hyper-reflexivity become increasingly similar to the means of music criticism. A schizophrenic hyper-reflexivity thus creates a place of empathy between the experience of schizophrenics, the work of Conceptual music, and also the work of music criticism. Because of the nature of the works examined and the medium of that examination (i.e. schizophrenia and its action of hyper-reflexivity), this miming creates an object that refers not only back to the subject (e.g. George Brecht's work) but also reflects on the materials (i.e. the mode or vehicle of criticism). As a consequence, texts that serve as an analysis of works of Conceptual music can no longer retain their sense of distance from the work; they are forced to reflect on their own nature too. In doing that, these texts become reflections of the nature of their subjects, perhaps even embodiments of them – a real *phenomenological* understanding.

Another schizophrenic symptom that relates specifically to music is the experience of auditory hallucinations. As has already been discussed, the medium of Conceptual art is the idea. Ideas are understood to be lingual entities; therefore, the medium of Conceptual art is inevitably language-based. For works of Conceptual music, one might imagine that the aural properties of spoken language would come to be the focus; however, the focus remains on written language in these pieces. This serves to fulfill the requirement in Conceptual music of a complete break from all traditional mediums of music including (and especially) perceptual qualities of sound. One facet of schizophrenic experience is the auditory hallucination. These auditory hallucinations appear to be an aural representation of the voice of the thoughts of the sufferer. Indeed, 'thoughts-out-loud' is one term for a common type of schizophrenic hallucination. In this sense, schizophrenia is presenting the means of a Conceptual music here: the experience of ideas made aurally perceptible in the mind of the listener. This comes about via the process of hyper-reflexivity, i.e. stepping back to listen to one's thoughts rather than to live them. Some theories of the basis of these hallucinations characterize them as the presentation of the dialogue of one's own thoughts as if they are spoken aloud and come from outside the self (Evans et al., 2000; Gould, 1949; Green and Preston, 1981). In a situation where hyper-reflexivity on the nature of thought or on the 'internal self' has removed all feeling of attachment to any inner dialogue, this kind of dislocation makes some sense. Indeed, these auditory hallucinations often take the form of two voices, one commenting on the truthfulness of the other's propositions or evaluating them in the light of another perspective. This process of splitting the self or of stepping back from oneself to the point of losing sense of self sounds somewhat like the process involved in attempting to be an objective critic. Indeed, the conversations that go on between different critical 'selves' in the footnotes of academic texts or between texts and their footnotes and appendices, often reflect something of the nature of auditory hallucinations in schizophrenic experience.

The final example I will give here is perhaps the most obvious with relation to criticism, and that is schizophrenic language-use. Schizophrenic language-use often appears to follow certain rules that are based on what could be conceived of as the musicality of words rather than the standard rules of grammar, syntax and word-definition. For example, one peculiarly schizophrenic language trait is the use of words because of their aural properties rather than their usual set of meanings. Homonyms hijack sentences by swivelling them around pivot points. Rhyme becomes an organizing principle. Where conventional language cannot describe particular other-worldly experiences or concepts, neologisms are created to 'sound' the concept. Such behaviours can obviously be related to the project of creating a form of criticism out of written language that can simultaneously exist as music. All of the Conceptual music works I have examined so far with relation to my schizoanalytical practices are based on some form of language or language play. For example, Brecht's *Events* are all word scores, littered with puns and comic use of language and Cage's *Mureau* or *Emtpy Words,* are also pieces formed out of a schizophrenic-like experimentation with texts.

Examples of Schizoanalysis in Practice

Before concluding, it might be helpful for me to outline a brief example of my own schizoanalyses and what they might look like or consist of. This is difficult because schizoanalysis is an act rather than a description. One can't summarise any results, or make a conclusion. The work exists as an embodiment of its effect. Therefore it generally needs to be present in its entirety before that effect can be experienced. However, for the purpose of this article, it might be pertinent to give a flavour of the means by which this effect is sought, in order to give a further insight into the methodology.

My first attempt at schizoanalysis was based around George Brecht's score *Two Umbrellas,* taken from his collection *Water Yam,* for which, the score simply consists of two words, 'Umbrella, Umbrella' (1963):

> *The umbrella of umbrellas. The umbrella to end all umbrellas. The umbrella of one's dreams, so to speak. An umbrella that would so represent all umbrellas, other umbrellas would cease to have meaning; ghost umbrellas. An umbrella that those with umbrellas would experience umbrella envy for. How would this umbrella look? An umbrella of what proportions? How umbrella-like? Very like an umbrella or an atypical umbrella? We all know umbrellas, all have experienced umbrellas. We have walked under umbrellas, sheltered with umbrellas, shared umbrellas, wrestled umbrellas, dodged the rogue umbrella. Troublesome umbrellas, broken umbrellas, umbrellas with eyes, automatic actions, layered umbrellas, umbrellas like walking sticks, carved umbrellas. I had an umbrella canopy with LED stars once. An umbrella gift from an umbrella-loving friend. The umbrella-stealing taxi driver drove off with that umbrella in the back seat. I called to reclaim my umbrella from the umbrella department and they had many lost umbrellas but no umbrella matching my umbrella description. I was umbrella bereft. I mourned that umbrella. The umbrella of my dreams. A significant umbrella. Dream-umbrella.*

Years ago, while I was an undergraduate psychology student, I recall that 'umbrella' was the word chosen by a psychology lecturer to demonstrate the phenomenon of 'semantic satiation' to my class. He repeated that word over and over again for an uncomfortably long period of time. His intention was to tire it out, to satiate our minds with umbrella sounds. When semantic satiation occurs it results in a moment when a person no longer recognizes a word that he or she previously knew well. During my lecturer's demonstration for example, we listeners began to be confused as to whether the word 'umbrella' was the *right* word, the *real* word, whether it really meant what we thought it meant and sounded the way we had thought it ought to sound. We asked ourselves, 'do you *really* spell umbrella that way?'

There are certain words that induce this feeling more readily than others and it might seem that the more everyday and pedestrian the word, the more quickly this feeling emerges. Perhaps the word 'umbrella' was chosen by my lecturer because the umbrella is such a quaintly normal object from the austere days of 1907 when this phenomenon was first scientifically addressed (Severance and Washburn, 1907: 182–186). Perhaps it was used because it seems a slightly uneasy word in the first place, unyielding of its roots (at least that is how I have always thought of it). Perhaps it was the last object he saw before he entered the lecture theatre on a rainy Wednesday morning.

This experience with words is similar to what we occasionally experience with relation to other objects and things – something we call 'jamais vu'. This is the acute sensation or impression that one is seeing a situation for the first time, despite the rational knowledge that one has been in the situation before. Just as we have experienced occasionally in jamais vu, reality suddenly appears to be strangely altered in an inexplicable fashion at the outset of several kinds of mental health disorder, including schizophrenia. For the individual with schizophrenia, for example, not only words but also everyday objects begin to seem strange – somehow alien and enigmatic. In losing their normal everyday meanings, these objects therefore come to be strangely significant – imbued with what is called 'fugitive significance'. Colours become brighter and more 'experienced'; objects more definite; sounds more distinct and intriguing; people become ghostly and statuesque; experiences become significantly heightened or so unreal that they feel like no experience at all. It is a dream-like state where the world is stripped of its normal meanings. One schizophrenic patient has described it thus:

> When, for example, I looked at a chair or a jug, I thought not of their use or function – a jug not as something to hold water and milk, a chair not as something to sit in – but as having lost their names, their functions and meanings; they became 'things' and began to take on life, to exist […] I said: 'chair, jug, table, it is a chair'. But the word echoed hollowly, deprived of all meaning (Sechehaye, 1970: 55–6).

Another explained:

> Noises all seem to be louder to me than they were before […] I notice it most with background noises – you know what I mean, noises that are always around but you don't notice them […] it makes it difficult to keep your mind on something when there's so much going on that you can't help listening to (McGhie and Chapman, 1961: 104–5 cited in Siegel and West, 1975: 65).

The concept of immediate spontaneous and overwhelming meaning arising without effort from perceptual experiences as ordinary as a milk jug on a table, or the sound of a dripping tap, is extremely interesting. Indeed, Arthur C. Danto describes the very process of the creation of art very similarly in fact, describing it in the title of his influential philosophical work on the nature of art as the 'transfiguration of the commonplace' (Danto, 1981).

An umbrella one can't help listening to.

Conclusion

It is both freeing and challenging to write schizoanalyses. On the one hand, the development of these schizoanalytical texts has allowed me to use a more holistic writing process than previously, utilizing the strongest aspects of my creative musical compositional processes as an integral part of my academic research and writing. It has involved my reflecting on both music and text in completely new ways, for example: thinking about which aspects of an academic text might be considered or experienced as musical and how these might be brought to a reader's attention; contemplating conceptual manipulations in terms of rhythm, movement, contrapuntalism or even timbre; assessing musical meta-aesthetics; thinking primarily about *effect*.

It has also been a challenging process. Not only do I need to write about academic theory and create rigorous research, isolating and describing important aspects of how a piece works, but I also need to develop ways of demonstrating that effect with the text. This is quite a task. There are pitfalls in several directions, not least in over-describing something that should be left to experience, or, on the contrary, in abandoning the writing to creative processes and allowing it to stray out of the bounds of that which could conceivably be called criticism or analysis.

Ultimately, however, it is extremely gratifying to be able to find a way of writing about pieces, like those of Conceptual music, that seem to be resistant to the process of analysis. It is also appealing to be able to create musical listeners out of academic readers and to create music where previously there was none.

Notes

1 Edward Lippman, in his *Aesthetics Reader*, defines Conceptual music along these lines: via its effect on the traditional understanding of the nature of music through its questioning of the boundaries of music, and where that questioning is, 'an integral part of the musical experience and thus impossible to overlook or ignore' (Lippman, 1990: 419).

2 My use of the word 'object' here is wide, and in the context of the phrase the 'art object'. For example, I also here include actions or thoughts that are presented as works of art. 'Object' has never been a helpful term to use in describing music, where the terms 'piece', 'work' or 'composition' are more frequent and take into account the immaterial nature of the form.

3 In the past, music frequently served as the basis for discussion on the limits of philosophical knowledge and meaning, and was often used as an example of, 'a kind of discourse of the unsayable par excellence' (Scherzinger, 2004: 263–4).

4 Key texts in these areas include the early work of feminist musicologists and the work of those in gender studies, for example: *Opera: the Undoing of Women* by Catherine Clément (1988), *Feminine Endings* by Susan McClary (1991), *Musicology and Difference,* ed. Ruth Solie (1993), and *Queering the Pitch,* Philip Brett, Elizabeth Wood and Gary C. Thomas (eds) (1994).

5 Deleuze and Guattari describe a split between, 'schizophrenia as a clinical entity' and the 'schizophrenic process of deterritorialization': 'The major line ends at the body without organs, and there it either passes through the wall, opening onto the molecular elements where it becomes in actual fact what it was from the start: the schizophrenic process, the pure schizophrenic process of deterritorialization. Or it strikes the wall, rebounds off it, and falls back ... getting caught up in the asylum aggregate of paranoia and schizophrenia as clinical entities [...]' (Deleuze and Guattari, 2004a: 311)

References

Art-Language (eds) (1969/2000) 'Introduction to Art-Language: The Journal of Conceptual Art', in A. Alberro and B. Stimson (eds) *Conceptual Art: A Critical Anthology*, pp. 98–104. London: MIT Press.

Battock, G. (1969/2000) 'Painting Is Obsolete', in A. Alberro and B. Stimson (eds) *Conceptual Art: A Critical Anthology*, pp. 88–9. London: MIT Press.

Brecht, G. (1962/1963) 'Two Umbrellas', from *Water Yam*. Detroit: The Gilbert and Lila Silverman Fluxus Collection.

Brett, P., Wood, E. and Thomas, G. C. (1994) *Queering the Pitch: The New Gay and Lesbian Musicology*. New York: Routledge.

Cage, J. (1998)'Mureau', in *M: Writings '62-'72*, pp. 35–57. London: Marion Boyars.

Clément, C. (1988) *Opera: or the Undoing of Women*, trans. B. Wing. Minneapolis: University of Minnesota Press.

Danto, A. C. (1981) *The Transfiguration of the Commonplace: A Philosophy of Art*. Cambridge, MA: Harvard University Press.

Deleuze, G. and Guattari, F. (2004a) *Anti-Oedipus: Capitalism and Schizophrenia*, trans. R. Hurley, M. Seem and H. R. Lane. London: Continuum.

Deleuze, G. and Guattari, F. (2004b) *A Thousand Plateaus: Capitalism and Schizophrenia*, trans. B. Massumi. London: Continuum.

Evans, C. L., McGuire, P. K. and David, A. S. (2000) 'Is Auditory Imagery Defective in Patients with Auditory Hallucinations?', *Psychological Medicine* 30(1): 137–48.

Glass, J. M. (1993) 'Multiplicity, Identity and the Horrors of Selfhood: Failures in the Postmodern Position', *Political Psychology* 14: 255–78.

Glass, J. M. (1995) Shattered Selves: Multiple Personality in a Postmodern World. New York: Cornell University Press.

Godfrey, T. (1998) *Conceptual Art.* London: Phiadon.

Goldie, P. and Schellekens, E. (2010) *Who's Afraid of Conceptual Art.* London: Routledge.

Gould, L. N. (1949) 'Auditory Hallucinations and Subvocal Speech', *Journal of Nervous and Mental Disease* 109: 418–27.

Green, P. and Preston, M. (1981) 'Reinforcement of Vocal Correlates of Auditory Hallucinations by Auditory Feedback: a Case Study', *British Journal of Psychiatry* 139: 204–8.

Jameson, F. (1984/2000) 'Postmodernism, Or the Cultural Logic of Late Capitalism', in M. Hardt and K. Weeks (eds) *The Jameson Reader,* pp. 188–233. Oxford: Wiley-Blackwell.

LeWitt, S. (1967/2000) 'Paragraphs on Conceptual Art', in A. Alberro and B. Stimson (eds) *Conceptual Art: A Critical Anthology,* pp. 12–17. London: MIT Press.

Lippman, E. A. (1990) *Musical Aesthetics: A Historical Reader. The 20th Century,* Vol. 3, 3rd edn. New York: Pendragon Press.

McClary, S. (1991) *Feminine Endings: Music, Gender and Sexuality.* Minneapolis: University of Minnesota Press.

Osborne, P. (1999) 'Conceptual Art and/as Philosophy', in M. Newman and J. Bird (eds) *Rewriting Conceptual Art,* pp. 47–65. London: Reaktion Books.

Piper, A. (1993/2000) 'The Logic of Modernism', in A. Alberro and B. Stimson (eds) *Conceptual Art: A Critical Anthology,* pp. 546–9. London: MIT Press.

Sass, L. (1992) *Madness and Modernism: Insanity in the Light of Modern Art, Literature and Thought.* Cambridge: Cambridge University Press.

Sass, L., Parnas, J. and Zahavi, D. (2011) 'Phenomenological Psychopathology and Schizophrenia: Contemporary Approaches and Misunderstandings', *Philosophy, Psychiatry and Psychology* 18(1): 1–23.

Scherzinger, M. (2004) 'The Return of the Aesthetic – Musical Formalism and its Place in Political Critique', in A. Dell' Antonio (ed.) *Beyond*

Structural Listening? Post-Modern Modes of Hearing, pp. 252–78. London: University of California Press.
Sechehaye, M. (ed) (1970) *Autobiography of a Schizophrenic Girl*. New York: New American Library.
Severance, E. and Washburn, M. F. (1907) 'The Loss Of Associative Power in Words After Long Fixation', *American Journal of Psychology* 18: 182–86.
Siegel, R. K. and West, L. J. (eds) (1975) *Hallucinations: Behavior, Experience and Theory*. London: Wiley.
Solie, R. (ed) (1993) *Musicology and Difference: Gender and Sexuality in Music Scholarship*. Berkeley: University of California Press.
Ulmer, G. (1992) *Applied Grammatology: Post(E)-Pedagogy from Jacques Derrida to Jospeh Beuys*. Baltimore, MD: John Hopkins University Press.
Ulmer, G. (1998) 'The Object of Post-Criticism', in H. Foster (ed.) *The Anti-Aesthetic: Essays on Postmodern Culture*, pp. 93–126. New York: The New Press.
Woods, A. (2011) *The Sublime Object of Psychiatry: Schizophrenia in Clinical and Cultural Theory*. Oxford: Oxford University Press.

Eyes! Birds! Walnuts! Pennies!

Erin Soros

(Note: lines in 9 pt font are to be read aloud in a whisper, but as if you are trying to scream.)

Section 1. Stove

To: vvexer@hushmail.net

Subject: Lecture

Vlad,
See you Tuesday: Looking forward to your talk – I've never heard you present your work in pubic.

I was in a rush. *Public,* I meant – not *pubic:* I caught and corrected the typo, but first forwarded the e-mail to a friend as an example of the kind of slip that can emerge whenever I'm aiming to be suitably academic.

Wonderful, my friend responded, and were you planning to take *pubic* transportation?

Our e-mail exchange is dated the 24th of October, when these kinds of errors in language still seemed laughable and easy to share.

I arrived at the talk, sat in the front row. Flap of raincoats and notebooks as we settled in to listen. The dark pressed its face against the windows. The topic was liberty. My colleague is a philosopher. Russian. He spoke in a shorthand that others in the room seemed to grasp.

You mean props, I asked, as in theatre? He meant props as in propositions.

My colleague's words kept spitting, I mean splitting – was the problem his accent, I wandered? When I tried to pose a question, I couldn't seem to say what I meant without taking mistakes. Missed takes. Miss stakes. The stakes weren't that high – I was simply a member of the audience, as you are now sitting in front of me, and so if I didn't undertake, I mean understand, umbrella stand – I mean hear, if language had begun to slide, no one could really tell.

Then something snagged. What was it? – something bothered me about the content of the talk, and yet I couldn't quite articulate the trouble. My colleague's argument seemed to rely on a belief in someone who knew who he was and could control what he meant. I wanted to challenge this assumption of self-transparency. For example, a man at my gym in New York once asked me if I used tampons. He was saying something else, now, wasn't he? But we can't – was this what I wanted to say? – we can't speak what we want… or we can't say what we hear… or...

In my purse was an envelop full of receipts I was supposed to have submitted to the finance office for reimbursement. I'd procrastinated with the receipts, and was disturbed to find that the ink had faded so that each receipt was now blank. After the question and answer period, my colleague and I walked into the hallway and I showed him the receipts. He is a helpful sort of man. What did he think I should do? He too could see that the numbers had faded.

How strange, he said.

Their blankness seemed somehow significant. Nothing could speak for nothing.

Section 2. Way

Time is sitting on a chair.

How long did Friday go?

Hours and the air grew thick.

Section 7. Exclude

The next day was a few days later and I phoned another colleague because I could not remember how banks work. I was having trouble, I said, with cultural difference.

Are British blanks the same as Canadian?

I knew they held money, and I knew that what came out needed to balance with what came in, and I knew that my rent in the fabric was due on Monday, but I could not remember how to make the Balanchine. She said she was worried about me. I walked to her house – she lives on Gloucester Street. The number of her house is 65 – I remembered – but I could not remember how numbers go up or down.

I stood on the corner of Gloucester Street trying to recall who he was. In *King Lear* – Gloucester, Gloucester, I was sure it was *King Lear*. Was he the one who put out his own eyes? I thought I needed to remember this part of the play – if I were going to be able to use the street, to find my way along the street to her house. The play was the thing. This was how streets worked.

Section 3. Blinking

Saturday. Halloween. When I reached the bank I told the teller I had a migraine and couldn't look at numbers. This summed a good strategy. She was very sympathetic – her mother suffered from migraines too. Yes, I said, very painful. Migraines. Your loss, my grain. Can you tell me – I began to speak very carefully, as if stearing a car backward alongside a cliff. If I put this check into the bank, will I have enough to cover my rent on Monday? I held my head. She checked the standing order. She checked the balance.

Yes, she said, you're fine.

4. Temporary

I saw children walking down the street in their costumes. I saw a couple dressed in crazy hats – I recognized them only after they'd passed, but when I turned around to say hello, they were gone. They might have slipped indoors. I wasn't sure if I'd seen them after all.

On my coffee table sat Sebald's novel. I can't read the title. On the cover is a photograph of a blond boy in a white satan jacket holding a white stain hat topped with a feather. The boy in the phonograph could be on the way to a costume party. Perhaps he is dressed this way only for the camera.

5. Pump

The ancient Celts believed that the border between this world and the otherword became thin on the night we now call Halloween. Spirits (both harmless and harmful) can pass through.

Do you remember watching the movie *Halloween* when you were a teenager?

I sat in the living room. Time grew humid.

Just days ago words had worked. How many days before. I had been a writer talking on the phone about a film. The film was about me. They do these kinds of things in Canada. They make films about writers that no one would ever want to watch. I'm world famous in Canada. In Ottawa, which is a very dull place, they were going to screen the film and give me an award for a work I had yet to write. On the phone I asked when the award would be announced. It was a matter of security – would the public know in advance? I had reason to be concerned. I'd been receiving unwanted e-mails from a man who tracked my public presentations. I had reason. No use getting excited. For five years now this man has sent e-mails. I block them on one system and he finds another way through and I block them again and they collect in junk files and I send them to the police in a small town in British Columbia where he lives and they say he isn't dangerous he just wants to marry me. In Norwich I send them to a police officer, the name's Cox, he said, he gave me his card. Inspector Richard Cox. Go by Dick, he said. I forward my stalker's e-mails:

> Dear Dick Cox,
> I want to rove your breasts and be your guide to their voluptuousness.

My stalker is not very precise with his language. There are adjectives I could use to describe my breasts, and voluptuous is not one of them.

My stalker – he calls himself my stalker – he e-mails me to say he is not afraid of the police. He says he is not afraid of prosecution. He is itching for martyrdom.

He is going to get me pregnant.

6. Sandwich

My mobile rings. It is October 18th, two weeks previous, around 6 pm.

I answer in the bedroom. It is the coordinator of the award ceremony in Ottawa, where it is five hours earlier than it is here. She calls me to say she'd been thinking.

She has been thinking that I should not come to the ceremony.

We don't have the security, she says. This isn't Fort Knox.

He won't know I'm there, I say. I sit down on the bed.

You said he threatened you, she says.

I said his e-mails are threatening. There's a difference.

There's a danger, she says. The ceremony. It's on November 5th.

November 5th, I say, yes.

It's close to December 6th. She says. She has been thinking

But how would he know where I am? The sheets are twisted in my hand.

You would be putting everyone in danger.

I would?

Not just yourself, everyone in the room with you.

What are you saying.

There could be a copy-cat massacre.

14. Transcribe

On Halloween I sit and I think. In Canada we all know what December 6th means.

15. Bowl

Was there something I had missed?

November 5th could mean December 6th.

I scanned his e-mails.

I sat.

Copy cat

Fraidy cat

Cat got your tongue

Ridicule

Time can grow so humid it begins to spill.

Circulation

Behind the mustard, over on the shelf to the right – when I was fourteen I was stalked by a man named Derek who shot himself.

Very

Birdcage

The tradition of dressing up on Halloween stems from the belief that the mask will offer some protection. Will the disguise trick the evil spirits from finding you? Or is the act of doubling itself the protection, a way to frighten fear with fear? Perhaps the face is the real danger, and the mask just a way to hide our own violence. Thumb on the trigger. There are cracks in the cupboard, cracks in the air, a kind of sparkling like those evenings when my sister and I would shuffle socked-footed across the carpet and touch each others' elbows to pass electricity, shocks like small deaths.

I sit at the computer. I am logical. I read my stalker's e-mails. There may be some clue. Can words tell the future? I am putting too much pressure on words. They are starting to bend a bit. Look, they are starting to crack on the sides like the cupboard.

(How would he know? Who could he hurt?)

He could hurt my mother. For example, he has found my mother – this is what his e-mails say, although I know the woman he describes is not her. Furthermore, he says he saw her at a cultural event. No, you won't find my mother at one of those.

I am stalking your daughter, he says to this mother who is not mine. He says he is dressed as Marilyn Manson because it helps the brain that I have hurt.

I lie on my bed on my tangled sheets. I don't sleep. I think about my mother. If I don't sleep, if I keep thinking about my mother – this is what I used to think, lying awake below my sister in our bunkbed when we waited for the wide yellow arch of headlights to sweep through the house to tell us that our parents were home, smell of perfume and smoke and rum, a kiss on a face that is pretending to be asleep, if I think of my mother, if I can hold her in my head the entire time, there will be no accident. Girls, I think, secretly want to kill their mothers.

Hence the need to stay awake. So it would be an aggressive act, wouldn't it now, flying to this ceremoany in Ottawa to stand straight-backed in a blue dress and accept an award that he could discover and then find her, to reach me?

14. Turnip

Shut the window. The glass is damp on my fingertips. Fear clings to the sill.

Filth

The night tilts toward November. Safe. Safe soft sift. Breathe. Just breathe. I get up from my sheets and sit at the blue glow of the computer. I am fine. (The ceremony is in disguise as a wedding, or the wedding is in disguise as the ceremony.) I begin to write an e-mail to a man who once broke my heart in a small town in upstate New York. He is a philospher like my friend the Russian. He used to stand outside my office and make fun of how people put pennies in penny loafers. He laughed at my Heidegger jokes. He rubbed my office door.

I want to tell him now that I know where to meet him. At the ceremony doubling as a wedding!

Look I can close this door and open another one! Door number three! A wedding! Look, Ma, no hands! Magic! The light in the kitchen is protecting me! No award no film no stalker – how crazy of me to think once upon a time there was an award and a film and a stalker. It is not Halloween! I am feeling better, there is a fuller feeling in the kitchen, there is sitting at this computer composing an e-mail in the form of an alphabet, this seems important, the letters of the alphabet can reach out and find – my beloved! He'll know. He'll keep me safe.

I don't send the e-mail. I'm dreaming. I'm tilting toward the screen. The question mark is stuck. Each time I hit this key with a question mark, it gives me my initial. My initial in capital letters like a whisper that is shouting. Ē Ē Ē!!! My initial with an accent. Another language slips into this one. I remember the sound of the sliding wooden door of our kitchen. An orange haunting horrible sound meant supper is ready. *Egg ready* I used to shout. Ē Ē Ē! Whenever I type a question, it ends with my first letter. I am the answer!

The button on the sleeve of my jean jacket catches in the groove of the table. It tells me each time I am thinking something right. Type a few more words. Button catches. Something can pass through from this realm into the other one. There, see, it catches again. Ē Ē Ē ! Buttons! Gloves! That's what I need, a pair of white gloves to toss out the window. I surrender. I open the door to find the gloves I've tossed right out the window onto the pavement. The door sticks. Pull at the door – it sticks against the real, into the real, into the dark wide real outside inside no words, no letters! (No one is there!) The street is dark and blank. A styrofoam cup rolls in the wind.

If I could walk to Gloucester and spin in a circle he will appear. My beloved! Bring me pennies! Find Ē in the wedding!

Approximate

On Nov 2nd I make sure I am on time for my haircut.

A little off the edges, I say.

I can't cut your hair if you are holding your head, she laughs.

I let go of my head. Migraine, I say.

Pain. Killers. Make me nauseas.

Words walnuts the clock on the wall is showing my friend. I get up and run to the bathroom and pretend to throw up because time words images pressing on the roof of my mouth, the roof of my mind, code read in the bathroom broken bits like the pieces of cut hair that cling to chair legs.

Are you okay?

She stands smiling. Her blades in the air.

Sofa

That's the thing about that word – I never know when it is.

Whereas

Before I left for the hairdressers, on the morning of November 2nd, I made sure to leave a bag of walnuts, for my friend the philosopher. Russian. Props as in propositions. He was scheduled. Come over in the afternoon!

He was planning to help me with a grant application for a scholarship due November 2nd commemorating Dec. 6th., you know: Ēcole Polytechnique, violence against women, the fourteen.

I left them in the cupboard – you know the one, just inside the front door, before you come up the stairs to my apartment. It's where the landlord keeps the spare keys. You know, the place for walnuts. You know what they mean.

Ritual

My friend did not find the walnuts. He found me in my apartment with my new hair. He found me and he left me. He thought I should sleep. (If I sleep, she will die.) The next day he found me again and he took me to see Tom and they took me to see a doctor and I held my head. It hurts. Language hurts. If you try to make it speak the future then the words begin to crack.

They talk slowly, giving even emphasis to each syllable.

Two philosophers and a doctor. It takes three men to handle me.

Erin, we are just going to the hospital.

Just just just.

Jest as in a joke? Is this a joke wedding, or the real thing? Is the wedding at the hospital?

Just as in justice.

Just as in Jessica.

Do I know a woman named Jessica?

Will she be at the wedding?

Jess gist adjust her just her jester jodpur.

Faster

Fourteen. He was going to get me. He said it was going to happen.

Laundry

When I use the word talk, I mean stalk. I mean it's all wrong.

Time should stay where it is.

Stay.

Sit, time, sit. Time rolls over.

I didn't know that word. When I was fourteen. The word did not exist. There was nothing to call it. He did nothing to me.

What are you afraid of, anyway?

Then the years turned past December 6th, one year another year, each year December 6th came and left and meant not much at all until one year it meant what it means now in Canada one man took a gun and shot fourteen women.

You're all a bunch of fucking feminists.

Eyes

On the way to the hospital I show my friends all the billboards that are speaking to me.

See?

That one.

And that one over there.

Toward

Two philosophers walk into a psychiatric hospital. Flatscreen tv, cigarettes and yellow fingers, druel. She's allergic to milk, they tell the nurse.

I prefer Thai. But not up. Or get me nuts.

Erin, we are just.

If the philosophers weren't so worried about me, they might notice that language stretches taut like a clothesline. Or perhaps words hang on the line, and on one end the words just flap, they are sound and shape – YOU HAVE TRIED TO PUT TOO MUCH INSIDE THEM AND NOW THEY ARE SMASHED OPEN ON THE FLOOR! THEY ARE NOT CLOTHES! THEY CAN'T STRETCH! THEY ARE HARD BITS OF CURVES AND LINES SHATTERED! YOU ARE GETTING SPLINTERS IN YOUR FINGERS! SOMEONE GET A BROOM! SHE IS MAKING A HORRIBLE MESS! – and on the other end of the line the words go right on your body, *right into your body,* into your mind like those two pennies stuck to the book shelf in my hospital room! That button caught on the groove of the table! The arch of that seagull flying through the sky!

Another

We are wearing slippers. We are slippers! try oh try trick tricycle spoke wear on the stairs fire frayed my mascara mass acres and acres of mass hup hup house help HURT pen bird he is a white bird pen face knees and nuts and walls tie thai the walls

fall

fall

fall

Reinforcement

November 5th Lights. Camera. In the hospital they present my papers. Section two. Door number four.

Three. Men hold her down. It takes three.

Scream.

No words.

She brings out the needle.

The drug is labelled *danger.*

I am putting everyone in this room.

She lifts the needle and he lifts my nightgown my bare bare bottom.

In the future I will tell an audience and they will believe me! Won't they

believe me?

Thumb on the plunger.

penetration

blank.

Just Words

Erin Soros

Transcript of Author Interview, which took place in front of a live audience at *Reading Between: An International Festival of Creative-Critical Literature*, June 28, 2012, Montréal, Canada.

Hosted by Eleanon Kachtel, to be re-broadcast at a future date on *Writers and Readers, Ltd.*, CBC radio.

For audio: www.readingbetween.ca/justwords/don'tbother.Erin.ca.www.

Eleanon: I first came to know Erin Soros through her academic writing: her articles weave together psychoanalysis and philosophy to address contemporary crises. Then I came to know her through her fiction – evocative stories of loggers on Canada's West Coast. In fact, at one point I thought that there were two writers, each called Erin Soros, each working in a different realm. But as the performance we have just seen today illustrates, this particular Erin Soros crosses thresholds between the fictive and the non-fictive, the creative and the critical, the sane and the mad – all while asking us, as readers, listeners, and viewers, to rethink how tidy these divisions might be.

Erin Soros, I want to thank you for the performance of 'Eyes, Birds, Walnuts, Pennies' – it's unusual to see a writer not just read but perform her words. What inspired you to write the piece as a performance rather than something to be read 'straight'?

Erin: Sorry, I think there is something wrong with my mike. Okay, thank you.

Eleanon: Can you hear us both now? Yes? Okay, I was asking how do you think the piece works differently if read or performed? What dimension does the performance add?

Erin: I suppose I would have to ask you that.

Eleanon: Well, for us...for me...there was a sense at the end that you were *unreading* the text: you spoke what sounded in fact like a stream of nonsense, then the word 'fall,' we could hear that, clearly, you repeated it, and yet – and I am sorry that those listening at home would not have seen this – you were physically tipping, as you spoke. Even hearing you, I think the listeners could sense the words fall.

Erin: Okay, yes, I'm interested in what it means for us as humans to be born into language, which is itself a kind of fall – a post-Edenic state in which we are never truly speaking the object of our desire. Though we think we do. Some of us more than others. We are all stalkers, in that sense. When we say 'I want you,' 'I know you,' or even or especially 'I love you' – to say such a sentence is strangely a negation of who the other is, *as other*. It is saying, in a way, *you are who you are to me*. Who wants to hear that?

And yet we do – we want to be known, seen and heard, perhaps even read – by the beloved.

Here I'm also interested in the ordinary and yet extraordinary ways we 'fall' – we fall in love; we fall pregnant; we fall apart. I hoped to make falling exist in this piece not simply as a conceptual figure, but also as an affective experience, so the audience feels the vertigo. By 'unreading' I sense you mean those sections toward the end where language begins to work in increasingly non-referential ways – I might call it a falling, or perhaps an unjoining, to turn inside-out one of Heidegger's terms. I use the word 'bird' for example, but by that moment in the performance you may suspect I don't mean 'bird' as object, a flying thing, but perhaps just the sound of the word, the way it rhymes with word. Or perhaps it is a man's name.

It could be – Mike is. Who knows? Or I use the word 'mascara,' and then move quite quickly to 'massacre,' and to mass, and acre – you hear the word 'mask' too, in that combination – and so even as you are reading, or in this case hearing the text, there is a kind of falling away of what you think you are grasping in the words. In grave states of mental illness, one can experience what is clinically called `word salad`- a floundering that is alternatively jubilance and terror, in which language fails to make sense because its associations become indefinite and out of control. Sounds and meanings echo, syllables shimmering like water, becoming everything, becoming nothing. As a moment of communicative failure, psychosis might tell us something about the structure of language itself. Deleuze and Guattari speak of texts that make language stutter. My text begins stuttering, begins with what Freud might call a lapse— we all have lapses in speech and hearing, in the most banal ways, on a daily basis— but then the text travels to those threshold states when our experience of word and world is no longer 'just' stuttering, but truly falling through language, and hence through time and space.

Elenor: I love the climactic bit at the end, about words on the line, where at one end they are sound and shape and on the other they go right into your body and mind - can you say more about these striking images?

Erin: Well, on the one hand, words, they are things. If you are well-trained as a literary critic, you attend not just to the meaning of words in a poem, but to their sound, even their shape. So it is a kind of mad reading. Truly, you learn to read in an insane way – and I don't mean this in a cynical or derogatory sense. In a poem you read 'sun' and hear 'son.' Or you read Shelley and attend to what his words are doing to the sound of your breath. So you are attending, a bit too much, to the matter of language.

There is a symptom in schizophrenia, I forget what it is called, clang associations, I think, when speech becomes entirely sound, an echo of sound. I've also heard it called echolalia. Toddlers repeat words in that way. Poets experience this attention to rhythm and echo, but they contain it, or at least poems do, almost. But it can be a sign of mania, even or especially in a poet. So they do not get a free pass, apparently, those poets. You know, if you start going on about microphones and zylophones and ice cream cones, someone might worry.

Yes we *do* have to listen to language, or see it, in order to be able to read, but if we listen too well, or look too hard, it starts to be music or noise or the letter *t* can look like a cross or a table – and that is not what is supposed to mean. It is just a letter. So we have to lose the physicality of language in order for it to work.

Yet if we go to the other extreme, and see it as meaning, as if the word held the meaning, itself, transparently, that it was a nice little sense-nugget, no bones or gristle, and we our ourselves little self-nuggets, and this thing meaning can go right to us, right into us, with no translation by means of sound and image, with no need to refer through its spatial and temporal relationships, then it does not work anymore, really, it is not language. It is transcendence. So if we think we have some secret claim to the meaning of a word – for example, if we think it speaks only to us, and we are God or it is – then we are mad.

To make language work – to function sanely within our daily alphabet – we must constantly be negotiating a realm of meaning between these two poles: we use a word by limiting its association, and then we direct words at each other, even though we know we can never really hold them or make them hold.

I wonder if trauma upsets this balance, somehow.

I expect you too have had the experience of hearing bad news, and yet when you hear it you...cannot make the word mean – it stays its sound. Does that happen to you?

Or to go to the other extreme, you are grieving someone and you magically begin to find their meaning in everything, to see that person in all signs. Clinically that experience is called an *error of reference.* That joke you just overheard – it is as if he is speaking to you through it. And the billboard...it is talking to you. Subjectively it feels as if a word or perhaps gesture were saying something to you alone.

Eleanon: (Clears throat). I do think we felt that vertigo, as you read. I wasn't sure at first if the mistake was mine or yours – if I'd mis-heard a word, or if you had mis-read it, and if that was accidental or on purpose.

Erin: Yes, and then you make the accident signify – perhaps because you assume there is an author behind the text, which is a fair enough assumption because I'm in the room. Sometimes I call attention to the slips and sometimes I don't – and I'm sure that the audience might hear mistakes that I haven't actually made, because some people in this room will be listening through an accent, will be hearing me speak English but might also hear homonyms in their first language, what we call in English 'false friends.' So you might hear those, your brain would pick them up, and you have to make a decision about whether or not they signify – whether the doubleness, the difference, is meaningful or not. The same goes with the mistakes. Now if you start to read the world that way – if, for example, you read the signage on the side of a bus that just happens to cross your lane as you are sitting inside another bus and you are reading this text, and that signage works somehow, referentially, by chance, with this text, and you read that connection as a kind of private joke, that can be delightful, if you get the joke. If you think on the other hand that there was an author behind that moment, within the text, if you think the accident signifies through intent, then you are not getting the joke. You are schizophrenic. Sorry.

Eleanon: Are you in on the joke, here? You use the name 'Erin.'

Erin: Yes, I use my own name. But then there are many of us. Erins, I mean. Fictive, true, in sickness and in health, for better or perhaps worse. I'm one of those narcissistic people who wish I were the only one. Comes with the name, I think.

I performed this text at an academic conference, and afterwards, at the dinner, a woman whose own name I cannot recall, she accused me of appropriating the experience of someone who had fallen insane. It's a sign of disrespect – or theft, of suffering, is what she meant, I think. Hard to tell. This was between the soup and the entree. There is an experience, she implied, which this woman in my performance has endured and that I did not, I do not, and so I cannot grasp it and I shouldn't pretend that I can, that we can, not here, not in my words. Fair enough.

And I think the text fails precisely in this way, because I make it accessible, don't I? This Erin, these slips – it all seems understandable, and really what is happening to her, in the end, exceeds what we can understand, or at least certainly exceeds what language can hold. So there is something unutterable which I fail to represent.

But then there she is. The words are all you get.

Eleanon: Now that's something else: There is some word play clearer when reading - and some when speaking - why do this? Who is it for?

Erin: Oh Eleanon, that should be obvious.

Eleanon: (Blushing) I...er...I should explain that...I have access to the written text, and the audience does not, and I notice that you create some errors that the audience will hear, and some that signify only on the page – as with 'ceremony.' She spells it *c e r e m o a n y.*

Erin: That's not fare! That's cheating! Now you are just giving it away. That was just between us.

Eleanon: Erin, but if they are...

Erin: supposed to pay for that!

Eleanon: But with moany, then, what are you doing here?

Erin: Being interviewed by Eleamoney Kackel, on national radio. I hope. Or this is one hell of a delusion. You might be in mine, or maybe I'm in yours. Or some kind of combination. *Follie à deux.* As it happens.

Eleanon: But in the specific sense – I am curious how that relates to this performance.

Erin: Yes, you are curious. You have done your research. I will give you that. But so have I. For example, in one interview you quote from the writer Jackie Kay who says that you can tell a relationship is over when they start quoting Martin Amis. In my experience, it has almost always been Nietzsche. Never mind Martin. It's quoting Nietzsche. Once he appears, it is game over.

I'll tell you another story. There was one guy I dated, in New York the city, not the state, or not the one of my fantasy, that guy, his problem was not that he quoted philosophers, but that he could not. That bothered him, to be honest. It was a hang up. I could do it and he could not. And that was not the least of his worries. He told me once that when he was inside me, when he...er...needed to slow down, so to speak, he'd... think about the Queen. When he was inside me! The Queen! *But only when I wanted to slow down* – he always emphasized that, afterward, after he told me, like that was his defense. Like that would make me feel better. Like it was a compliment. So that is worse than Nietzsche or Martin Amis. I wish he could have been capable of thinking about them.

But the Queen.

Now whenever I look at her I think that's the closest I'll get to a threesome.

Eleanon: (Laughing. Begins to choke). Now you've lost me.

Erin: That's the risk. (Offers water.) Here, have a drink.

Eleanon: You use humour in the piece too...

Erin: Use, that's an interesting word, Eleanon. He used her, I use it – what am I using it for? Does it have to have a use value--where's my return?

Eleanon: That's what I was going to ask you.

Erin: We aren't getting very far. But it's your interview. I always wondered why it was called that. Our speech is going to be aired on the radio, where you don't view anyone. Interview – are we seeing between? Between what? Eleanon, have you ever been tempted to fake it?

Eleanon: Fake it?

Erin: I mean, if a writer cancels – just have someone play the part? Or you could. We can't see you. Or take me, for instance. I'm usually available.

Eleanon: I think we are getting off....

Erin: To be honest, Eleanon, I've never thought of you that way, but I can use my imagination. Do they allow that kind of thing at the CBC?

Eleanon: It would be heavily taxed.

Erin: Text?

Eleanon: You heard me.

Erin: That's interesting, because to say one is heard, one is implying a kind of herding, in the other sense. I just spelled it *h e r d*. There is a collective implied, in meaning. And in our definition of insanity. So if I said I believe Christ died and was risen, I'm free to speak. But if I say my beloved died and was risen, I'm tied down. In Canada at least. Or shot. One of these things is not like the other one. And this herding also determines how we experience and define crime. I make a play on 'stearing' – in the performance, though you can't see it when I'm speaking. I think it was an accident – I can't spell. There I'm giving something away. Text free. Which reminds me, what is that joke, in Canada, about Reading – how many miles from Reading? I'm now living in the UK – maybe 60, 80 miles from Reading – and now I know how it's spelled. Is it because the CBC used to have a broadcasting station in Reading? Is that it? I still don't get the joke.

Eleanon: I'll have to ask Michael Endright.

Erin: Right. Get to the bottom of that one. Is he single?

Eleanon: Back to crime. I know that audience members will wonder, as they hear this piece, what really happened? And don't we need to know? If this is a matter of law? Aren't you making an accusation?

Erin: Yes, *j'accuse*, but whom? And yes, perhaps it's all fine and good to play with language in this way, but how could I testify in court? If Erin is insane? What would happen? I'm interested here in who can be a witness. It's actually terrifying, if you think about it.

Eleanon: You mean once you've been....

Erin: Sectioned. (Shudders). Whenever I hear that word I always think of the opening to Foucault's *Discipline and Punish*.

Eleanon: As in quartered.

Erin: Exactly. You *are* well read, Eleanon. Glad they hired you.

Let us see: there's a kind of violence done to oneself, and one's word, when one is sectioned. From that moment forward. There is a new episode, a new beginning, or a new falling – in which the referential status of your language is now in question. More so than with others. I would claim. So you are no longer a witness. Not even to your own life.

There are two places that this particular Erin may honestly need to testify to the truth, no slipping: in the hospital and in the court. And in both locations, once you are sectioned your words no longer signify in the same way as another citizen's. If I am inside, say, and I said I was a writer, for example, and that I need to accept an award in Ottawawa – wouldn't that make me sound insane? A film made about me? I am an award winning writer! I am being followed! And I'm saying all this while wearing slippers?

Eleanon: Yes, as we are listening to you perform the text, you create a suspicion about what happened and what did not. Medically and legally. Is this all delusion, we wonder – was she stalked as a teenager, as she says? Is she being stalked now? Or is the present a delusion of the past? Or vice versa? And is she testifying to us from an imagined hospital – or perhaps in hope of a future testimony within the law?

Erin: Well, that is the problem. That's the anxiety. And you can hear that I don't want to quell it. As it happens. That sense of confusion is quite close to a delusional experience. Let them eat pretend cake.

Eleanon: But there are some things you reference that are real. The gradual unfolding of the significance of 'December 6th' is great - what is the purpose of anchoring the spiralling and spinning words and sections there?

Erin: Everyone knows that December 6th is real. At least, for those who speak English, and even for those who don't, they could look it up:

December? Check.

6th? Check.

So Dec. 6th signifies. They could say, with some assurance, that they know what it names. They could even point to it, if they had a calendar, preferably something free from the bank.

Of course, they may not know what it signifies in Canada.

Eleanon: Murder. Massacre

Erin: But if I were in a foreign country and I said I felt apprehensive about that date, just naming that date, I think my fear would be considered insane. And if I said, with some increased agitation, 'you know, you know what I mean – Dec 6th,' they wouldn't know. I could say again – *you know, the flowers on the lapel, the news anchor, the anniversary, polytechnique, the 14....* all these things that would speak to a Canadian, quite clearly, even when I'm circling round the referent, like this, well those words wouldn't necessarily speak to someone else. Not in that way. So when we are elsewhere, say, outside our own herd, there remains a shadow meaning, now, in that date, for me and for other migrant Canadians. So we are double-reading, or perhaps over-reading, and alone. If we are alone. With that meaning.

Eleanon: It wouldn't be lost on this audience. In Montreal. Dec. 6th.

Erin: No. Yes. Just as September 11th wouldn't be lost anywhere in the world. Not now. That date is the thing it names. Which is what it doesn't. Or can't. Odd, isn't it? The US has superpowers...

Eleanon: Erin Soros, I was wondering here what you were saying about fear, its communicability, and also its relation to crime.

Erin: Exactly.

Eleanon: It was a question.

Erin: It was a statement. You were wondering. So you were. It's not really up for me to agree or disagree. As I said, I don't know you. But to be honest I do find with you, Eleanon, that it always *is* a question, in the end, with or without the mark. Isn't it now? After all these years? I suppose you can't help it. It must be annoying to be married to you. Or are you single?

It's interesting that the word 'laugh' is 'fall' backward. Sorry – Elenor, that was not in the text. That just came to me.

To change the subject, to take the horse by the tail, so to speak, I tend to read backwards, given my last name is a palindrome, of course, where the mirror doesn't make any difference: coming or going, I am the same damn thing. A strange training.

But again and again stalking – and this is where it is wedded to trauma, which we cannot experience, or never in time – it takes place *between* the present of the threat and the future that will never arrive.

Eleanon: Never?

Erin: Well, it can arrive. The threat *can* arrive, of course, but then it's not a threat – then it's not stalking, right, it's another crime. Rape or murder – we use other words. It has another name. Something took place. So when police officers dismiss stalking, as they often do, even though we now have a word for it, and beyond a word, even though it now has a whole sentence, ten years even, in Canada, a long confinement – if the police still say, in the name of this crime, 'nothing happened,' they are of course write. I mean right. No one saw that.

Eleanon: What? (Coughs).

Erin: Never mind, here – have another drink. Nonnie – can I call you Nonnie? No? It doesn't matter. What I'm saying is that stalking is a fake intimacy, it's a crime drama as a love story, a false one. Or many. It's a crime of suspended reference. Stalkers often make threats through innuendo, or through quoting a text, for example, a short story in which the characters marry and die – stalkers seem obsessed by weddings, and unhappy ones, in the end. In truly odd ways. They must know there is no match. It certainly wasn't this Erin that his text described, even when he called me by my name, all of them. And he did that too, as if he knew me.

They don't name the violence directly, or not all of them do, no, not all the time. But it is there.

It's a crime that takes place in representation – through words, symbols, pictures. There can be acts, of course, sometimes – you might be literally followed. But that kind of action is not essential for the crime to take place. It doesn't need to take place. It's a crime in which nothing happens.

Eleanon: And here you mean...

Erin: Or don't. Yes. By the way, that's what my Mom calls 'readings.' Last night, for example, she called my hotel room to wish me luck. For today. I love you, she said. She always says that. And, Erin, good luck at your hearing. It's a reading, Mom, I corrected her. A *reading*. Not a hearing. I've told her before, but...

Eleanon: We're out of time.

Erin: ...that woman always has the last word.

Eleanon: She does.

It is in their Nature to Change
On Mis-leading

Elizabeth Reeder

When introducing the day at the Determining Form conference in June 2010, I attempted to give entrance to some points and counterpoints on the subject of Creative Non-Fiction. It was, and still is, my intention to provide some grist to the mill. Although, as I sit down to write that spoken introduction into a written essay, I'm aware of how my thinking has changed in the intervening months – unsettlings and settlings influenced by the reading, teaching, living and writing I've been doing since.

The term 'creative non-fiction', which seems to have such purchase in these discussions, continues to cause unease and I find it particularly problematic and disappointing that the essay – as a structure, a process and an idea – is somehow held captive within this contradictory and strangely closed term.

Creative Non-Fiction. The words themselves hold the seeds of my malcontent. Non-Fiction: it states, almost adamantly, that it is *not* fiction. But then place the 'creative' before it and the term indicates a desire to have the sexiness, the freedom (possibly, the considered craft and discipline) of fiction writing. The term Creative Non-Fiction can misguide readers, thinkers, and writers by setting the wrong expectations of what the writing will be or will convey because the term is caught up with universals like fact and truth and creativity – abstractions that are impossible to pin down, and yet tend to polarize.

This focus on dialectics opens up the practice of writing between forms (and between and beyond disciplines) to a lot of attacks about the importance of fact, and makers' allegiances to fact, as well as about the limitations of fiction, imagination and art in the construction, conveyance and acquisition of knowledge. Readers' thirst for 'fact' can also, crucially, make us forget other experiences we might have or seek out when we read a book or witness art or listen to music. The creation of an immediate, visceral experience can be connected to knowledge but is also, often, something beyond words and conscious understanding; sometimes when we read, we seek out escape or joy or immersion or entertainment, and these experiences are not necessarily devoid of meaning or fact or significance or truth. The creation of this sort of writing or art requires skill, talent and craft to produce. And it's this aspect of making and what we name what we make, that still garners my interest and my focus.

A false notion of what creativity can mean – like the perceived 'I can do anything' freedom of creativity – can lead to a devaluing, ignoring or undermining of the graft and craft of making and writing. Sometimes the 'creative urge' can be called intuition as if it comes from elsewhere and moves like a sort of magic, but for me intuition is about excellence and embodied knowledge and something that is learned and re-learned, practiced, applied and re-applied, in various ways at various times – intuition and instinct are ideas and skills we know so well they're second nature to us. They too emerge from periods of study and practice and shouldn't be taken for granted and need to be constantly challenged and adapted in order to remain rigorous and robust, as well as subtle, flexible and to hand to us as makers. Perhaps I am concerned that writing will not be viewed as a discipline but will rather be viewed as an escape from discipline and I'm not sure we're putting enough pressure on writers or readers to understand the power language, form and structure wield on a piece of writing.

My largest concern is that the phrase 'creative non-fiction' fails to draw our attention to what I think is always the most crucial element of any piece of writing, which is the writing itself. When we pay attention to the writing, we also become aware of what the writing itself makes possible. This is writing and reading beyond fact; this is, as I'll talk about later, writing, reading and thinking about knowledge in context.

at the top of mealle a buichaille

On the cusp of the new year, the blue of cold clings to the trees as hoar frost and in weak sun crystals sparkle but do not melt. I start to walk the steep ascent and am grumpy until I clear the treeline and head onto the bare shoulder. Here the Cairngorms fall into place around me: miniatured trees, black-grey rock and mirrored lochs and I unravel my scarf from around my neck, tie it to my pack, and breathe in the sharp, nearly frozen air. At the top, squat reindeer have antlers like broken twigs and they nudge stones on the tundra to get to food, their slow chewing progression brings with it the clicking of small rocks, tendons over bones. I look in all directions, to the blue sky, to the clicking clattering ground and then, to the east, where the winter heather starts to take hold, there's a dog barking and pulling at his lead to be among the beasts. The wind blows, the sun is bright and weak, and just emerging from the brow of the hill appears a figure with wool layers and ruddy cheeks and I walk towards her and the dog pulling, pulling at his lead. When we hug we compress layers and layers of clothes, and the air, between us.

There are words for the kinds of spaces which exist between other places and a lot of them are about landscape like littoral, ecotone, twilight.

In between places there is something solid, a traveler, crossing over. The very details noticed in the midst of travel or shock or bewilderment can hold us fast; lost becomes found, the strange settles into a familiar.

> If he can walk. If he can support his weight. If he can make it, unaided, to the toilet. If he can remember what it was like to be here, in his house, curious. If only his favorite cereal would taste like it used to. If he could do his taxes. The world is round and the sun wakes him,

> often colorful before it is bright. There isn't a this or a that, assisted living or skilled nursing, it's a continuum, they say.
>
> We start this day with a conversation, talking about how he could walk out of rehab. This is where we end the day, 2mg of morphine, his dry lips, his closed eyes, until they are open and he asks what day it is and I tell him, it's valentines day, the fourteenth of February. Today is Sunday. Tomorrow is Monday the fifteenth. He closes his eyes. Sleeps. Maybe. Or drifts between places. A soft press of my hand to his chest, his bulky rib cage.
>
> This is to say I don't know. And I do. I am lost. I know how to be right here, as a daughter. I know this. And again and again I don't know what to do in the minute, to move us out of that minute and successfully into the next one.

Here in these places between lost and found I witness in silence and in deafening chaos and I make up stories that will be memories. Walking upon terra incognita love becomes grief and essay, poem. Each memory forges a new path and this writing acts like a magnet pressed to the face of my compass.

essaying

I carry a preference for using the word Essay, if forced to use a definition at all. 'Essay' does a lot of the heavy lifting for us. Defined simply as an attempt or a trial; it may also be thought of as a journey or as a verb, as John D'Agata writes about and exemplifies through the essays he includes in his books *The Next American Essay* and *The Lost Origins of the Essay*.

> Or: Maybe the essay is just a conditional form of literature – less a genre in its own right than an attitude that's assumed in the midst of another genre. (D'Agata, 2003: 41)

Make it a gerund, *essaying*, and it becomes graceful, moving like a dance. 'Essay' holds these definitions already within its domain. It doesn't give primacy to or draw undue attention to fact or to outcome, but encompasses within the idea of essay the process and final product for both the writer and reader.

How do we journey and how do we seek out knowledge? Anne Carson introduces her 'Anthropology of Water', which is a pilgrimage, a living grief, in this way:

> To look for the simplest question, the most obvious facts, the doors no one may close, is what I meant by anthropology. I was a strong soul. Look I will change everything, all the meanings! I thought. I packed my rucksack with socks, canteen, pencils, three empty notebooks. I took no maps, I cannot read maps – why press a seal on running water? After all, the only rule of travel is, Don't come back the way you went. Come a new way. (Carson, 2000: 123)

W. G. Sebald has a similar spirit of adventure in his process and in his writings,

> I never liked doing things systematically. Not even my Ph.D. research was done systematically. It was always done in a random, haphazard fashion. And the more I got on, the more I felt that, really, one can find something only in that way, i.e., in the same way in which, say, a dog runs through a field. If you look at a dog following the advice of his nose, he traverses a patch of land in a completely unplottable manner. (Cuomo, 2010: 94)

From this dog-in-a-field approach, his writings emerge into the world and feel like memories and dreams and listening to a knowledgeable grandfather or grandmother and they remain genre-less; the back cover of *The Rings of Saturn* states that the book is Travel, Memoir and Fiction, and if the rumours are true Sebald wanted his book to belong to all genres (*Patience [After Sebald]*, 2012).

In his recent exhibition *The Tomb of the Unknown Craftsman* at the British Museum Grayson Perry stated, 'I dress up, I tell stories, give meaning to things and make them a bit more significant. Like religion it is not a rational process, I use my intuition. Sometimes our very human desire for meaning can get in the way of a having a good experience of the world.' (Perry, 2011).

These examples manifest one of the greatest possibilities of essaying (and art), which is to allow the process's full scope to influence the outcome, and for that final form to be something other than what is familiar or comfortable or recognizable, something not solely bound by this pressure for singular meaning, or for usefulness (as it's commonly understood).

In some ways I am querying our need to name genre. Although a name can act as a guide, we often name a piece of writing in order make it safe, knowable, somehow ease the reading of it. Perhaps we think that by categorizing we can set up expectations so that it might be familiar to the reader (or more acceptable to institutions or markets) or that perhaps we're thinking that we might tame it. And I'm wondering if some writing may be damaged by placing it within a definition that places pressure (for instance, of truth and fact) upon it. I'm thinking particularly of more radical forms of essay, which cross-over and between so many forms and genres. Or of art where the name of the medium does not place this pressure upon a piece of art. Sculpture has no allegiance to fact, for instance. In this way, 'essay' gives us more options as writers and readers.

In this other medium, in this other genre, which already exists between genres and expectations, I'm wanting the practice of writing to be valued exactly for its imagination, craft, discipline as well as the knowledge it might convey. And there are long discussions to be had about the ethics and integrity of how closely we hold to reality, to ideas of facts and truths, and to instances where the bonds of trust between writer/reader/listener might be broken (an example of this is Mike Daisy's recent falsifications about Apple on *This American Life*, a programme which has a clear journalistic integrity, which led to a retraction and an hour long programme about just these issues [Glass, 2012]). So even in radical forms of writing there are expectations, facts and truths, emotional resonances, details both concrete and abstracted, and they are crucial to the writing and its effectiveness and its reception, and there's learning to be had, there's so much knowledge and enjoyment and ambiguity and resolution.

how we choose to travel

Writers and readers meet in moments of space that exist between other places, between genres, between life and death, and to essay is to attempt, is to journey. *Or: Maybe every essay automatically is in some way experimental – less an outline traveling toward a foregone conclusion than an unmapped quest that has sprung from the word* question (D'Agata, 2003: 95). The very details noticed in the midst of travel or shock or bewilderment can hold us fast and Virginia Woolf describes these instances as 'moments of being'. Anne Carson has her own way and writes in one of her elusive and illuminating introductions in her collection, *Plainwater*:

> The marks construct an instant of nature gradually, without the boredom of a story. I emphasize this. I will do anything to avoid boredom. It is the task of a lifetime. You can never know enough, never work enough, never use the infinitives and participles oddly enough, never impede the movement harshly enough, never leave the mind quickly enough. (Carson, 2000: 29)

In this wilderness some experience woods-shock or *jungle-fear* or awe and, like art, essay and poetry flourish under the expectations that they can do anything, be anything. In one of her Short Talks, Anne Carson introduces Parmenides, a philosopher poet, who comes to us in the form of some words surrounded by so much space (just like Sappho, so much of history, so many texts, so many absences) and this space generates possibility, interpretation and imagination. When I read about him the water calms quickly over the ripples he makes and I am left a sense of *something newly missing* (like when the water smoothes over Chicken Little in Toni Morrison's *Sula),* something held and carried by memory – that crafty, faulty, generous sense. As Anne Carson writes in this short talk 'On Parmenides':

> I fear we failed to understand what he was saying or his reasons. What if every time he said *cities,* he meant *delusion,* for example? (Carson, 2000: 32)

Names and categories often provide comfort. Nomenclature is meant to be a useful binding, like how swaddling a baby calms it. For some, these definitions simply bind a piece of writing to burdensome expectations, which limit the reading of it. Lydia Davis calls her short pieces stories, although other people have called her 'an essayist in a storywriter's drag' (Marcus, 2007 cited in Shengold, 2007: 38). Anne Carson calls her work Short Talks, sometimes, and some of her poems are essays, and her essays are poems. Some of us are saying that category doesn't matter as much as the words do, as much as the whole, as the experience of the whole.

Sometimes I am held by something that Lydia Davis might call fear, which exists between reality and what is imagined. She writes:

> Nearly every morning, a certain woman in our community comes running out of her house with her face white and her overcoat flapping wildly. She cries out, 'Emergency, emergency,' and one of us runs to her and holds her until her fears are calmed. We know she is making it up; nothing has really happened to her. But we understand, because there is hardly one of us who has not been moved at some time to do just what she has done, and every time, it has taken all our strength, and even the strength of our friends and families too, to quiet us. (Davis, 1998: 133)

In a good story everything that happens is pushed by something else, Anne Carson writes, quoting Aristotle. So I've brought us here because I listen too, to a wise man who said, never let facts get in the way of a good story. He was, of course, quoting someone else.

a plant called audacity

Craft and structure give any information or fact or idea or image contained therein a specific context; form binds knowledge to an image and syntax and shape and the fact/idea/ knowledge/image can no longer be simply extracted (not in good practice or in good conscience) but needs to be taken in context. Importantly, context is not only linked to the language and the form (through which knowledge is constructed and conveyed), but also created by each individual reader/learner who comes to each text and each image they witness, just as themselves, with their own prejudices and biases and needs (creative or critical). As John Berger writes in *Ways of Seeing*, 'We never look at just one thing; we are always looking at the relation between things and ourselves. Our vision is continually active, continually moving, continually holding things in a circle around itself, constituting what is present to us as we are.' (Berger, 1977: 9)

In my PhD thesis, I talked about a creative and critical topology as a way to understand how our needs as makers, thinkers and readers are not only inter-dependent, but how they change over time:

> [A] Creative and Literary Topology [is] an individual, lived and creative landscape (topography) that changes over time. The element of time inherently adds the requirement for change, adaptation, risk, failure and survival. As a maker you apply your own interests and needs to your explorations and how they map themselves in your own realm remains something that your own observations, reading, writing, practice, responsibility and risk will dictate. (Reeder, 2009: vi)

Makers continually push at and challenge what we think and know and attempt, and must take responsibility not only for the process, but also for the quality and nature of the final product.

The stronger the process and the structure (by this I mean, more it is interrogated and has its own integrity), the more dynamic this topology of experience, making and reading becomes. Poetry can exemplify this 'restraint as specificity', as illuminated by Lyn Hejinian:

> The investigation of how language works and how it conveys arrays of sense and meaning is a specifically poetic undertaking. In the course of it, one inevitably discovers that language in a poem does not lay down paths that are always simple to follow ... Knowledge [in a poem] is, in other words, transitive. It is also transient, though recurrent, occurring in situ, in experience. One doesn't know something constantly or continually, but only episodically, in the event. (Hejinian, 2000: 226)

A rigorous approach to essaying can shape the course of an exploration, can produce thinking and research of a different order, and can allow the process to be manifest in the final form in a way that encourages unconventional ways of approaching or thinking about the text and leads to the possibility of unexpected revelations, connections and outcomes.

When we essay, we have to change the expectations of readers who have been trained to read for facts. An essay should set out its stall early, give an entrance that embeds attention into each reader's approach to a text, a focus that pays attention to the whole piece, to the ideas and how they're offered up, their specific context, the reverberations they create, the way they make us look back to other texts and sources, as well as forward to new ideas or connections.

Grayson Perry approaches the complicated relationship between maker and reality, between what is made and what is found there, in this way, 'Do not look for meaning here. I am not a historian, I am an artist... Reality can be new as well as old, poetic as well as factual and funny as well as grim.' (Perry, 2011).

I would be remiss if I did not draw attention to the fact that the term 'essay' also has baggage and can be reduced by reader, writer and critic (and often is!) to mean something dry and academic, a piece of non-fiction once more shackled to fact and severed from the craft of language. Like Creative Non-Fiction, the essay has much to overcome before it can be a truly good guide. However, a strong essay will be one that is written well, which sets out its own parameters for consideration and judgement; and is a piece of writing in which each word and where it's placed, matters.

One of the great things about art, essay and poetry is that they contain infinite possibilities of form and content. Crucially, within this vast freedom exists a great responsibility for us as writers: to have practical, intuitive and applied rigour in our practice; to apply stringent as well as subtle critical reading and editing to our work and to the work of others; and to seek out and value deep and varied imaginings. No matter what it is titled or named or how people want to define it, it's this excellence of writing which proves a text's worth.

on embedded knowing and language

As Andrew Marr sketched the sun rising over the coast on his iPad, a daily practice temporarily borrowed from Hockney, he observered: 'The harder you look, the more you see and the more you get back.' This simple statement introduces the idea of attention, of how the length of time we spend observing something impacts what we can get back. This is even more true if this attention emerges from a strong creative practice and craft, or a concentrated experience of witnessing art. My suggestion is that the more time we spend, the more individual the looking becomes because what we observe intermingles with our own references, contexts, knowledge, ideas and emotions.

Inherent in the interest in, or ability to be comfortable within, the sort of unknowing that allows for multiple interpretations, is a nimbleness, and understanding and a valuing of the very changeable nature of words, language and meaning.

As Woolf writes, '[words] hang together, in sentences, paragraphs, sometimes for whole pages at a time. They hate being useful; they hate making money; they hate being lectured about in public. In short, they hate anything that stamps them with one meaning or confines them to one attitude, for it is their nature to change.' (Woolf, 1937)

Hejinian talks about language in a similar way:

> Language itself is never in a state of rest. Its syntax can be as complex as thought. And the experience of using it, which includes the experience of understanding it, either as speech or as writing, is inevitably active – both intellectually and emotionally. The progress of a line or a sentence, or a series of lines or sentences, has spatial properties as well as temporal properties. The meaning of a word in its place derives both from the world's lateral reach, its contacts with its neighbors in a statement, and from it's reach through and out of the text into the outer world, the matrix of its contemporary and historical reference. (Hejinian, 2000: 51)

Therefore:

> embedded knowing – it is knowing something in the context in which it is meaningfully known. It is conditional. A statement like

> 'I know sky' is vehemently subjective and apparently unconditional, but nothing we can know – or nothing that is real – is unconditional. (Hejinian, 2000: 220-1)

A strong essay understands the dynamic nature of language and makes its knowledge conditional. There's not a single reading of a sunrise, because we connect it to other sunrises we've seen, fictional sunrises, artistic renderings of sunrises; the colors take our thoughts to other images that share these colors, or they evoke emotions we perhaps don't have words for. The point is that our reaction to something as simple as a sunrise, isn't simple. We draw connections, it does not settle on just this day or this moment.

For me this realization leads to a question, for us as makers. After you look (and if I can stretch it to read, experience, hear …), what do you make, and how do you make it? How does what you make affect how others observe and see it? And how does what you make affect how you observe and read the world?

lost wax casting

A wricht builds coffins and cabinets and all sorts of things out of wood and often needs other objects to complete the task: lock and key, hinge, clasp; something to line the inside of the box. Seamstress wordsmith wricht. A tree becomes a boat or a door; and an old joist becomes a chair or something to place across the road for traction when the rains come on. In New Mexico, Walter De Maria forged lightning rods in New Mexico, needlesharp to seduce light and fire to the ground, and under his wooden table I place a single hand on your thigh and later there's a catching of hands as we walk through a lightning field with distance peaks creating and withholding stormclouds. Still later, here, our wedding band is plain, is what is turned and pressed and worried when in crisis, when in doubt, and home can be a foundry for if the band is lost or sold or melted down we are still left with the bond between us.

Genesis is a key pressed into butter, wax, something impressionable. It is clear like the bright call of waxwings as they trill from berry to branch in a clutch of days that can never be predicted. The beginning and the remembered. Remove it, cast it, palm it. Wait for the opportunity to put the key to use, and then pay attention as one surface communicates with another.

we are all readers

I'm suggesting that not only must we question the terms we use when discussing processes and writings that contain such infinite possibilities, but I'm drawing attention to the idea that how we read, how we make, and how we learn should be represented in the words we use to describe what we make. Naming can provide comfort and guidance and it can also include ambiguity and process and crossover. The concrete and knowable in what I'm talking about is the writing itself, the excellence of the writing, and writers and readers are in this space, between places and genres, in movement, and it is in their nature to change.

magnet to the face of a compass

In the spring of 1983, the Great Salt Lake rushed down the streets of a city after drowning birds' nesting grounds which had lain near its shores, and Terry Tempest Williams' mother was dying. Both events were inevitable and unconnected. In her book *Refuge: An Unnatural History of Family and Place,* the map of the Great Salt Lake is disorienting, north points west, west south, and you have to pay attention in order to find a familiar anchor. North of where I live, in the Black Cullins of Scotland, a compass will not work because the magnetic hills disrupt the heart of this simple object that gives direction.

When some people find themselves lost, they listen. Not all can handle the silence or the displacing but I have a feeling that the most exciting knowledge always contains some element that is not known and cannot be known. Some may find it hard to describe this space and therefore hard to value it: what cannot be named, cannot be proved. So we talk around it, root ourselves in details, and by talking around it, we leave space for art.

This year during fifteen days in February, I take notes even when I'm too tired. For a week I give myself a minute with my computer on my lap, to video a note of the day. My hair is up or down, glasses on or perched, and my eyes are sleep-filled. The last recording, just past midnight and into the nineteenth, is grainy, like an old film, filmed in the dark of his room. The small light on top of the bureau is not up to the job of illuminating. I whisper, and sometimes, in the background dad can be heard. This is all I will write of this night: how we listen.

As each return to a memory creates an original path through the brain, words act like a magnet pressed to the face of a compass. Sometimes love means grief and essay poem. Witness means words, perhaps a little bit of story. And sometimes essay means *a verb*, a journey, an entrance.

Acknowledgements

Some elements of this essay were previously published in *PN Review* 196 as 'between places: if, then, essay'.

John D'Agata has recently been pushing the boundaries of essay as art, about to be brought to light in the book *The Lifespan of a Fact*, published April 2012. As I cannot access the primary text and make up my own mind, I cannot include this in the discussion here. The Mike Daisy falsifications, provides a similar context for this discussion.

References

Berger, John (1977) *Ways of Seeing*. London: Penguin Books.

Carson, Anne (2000) 'Short Talks' in Anne Carson *Plainwater: Essays and Poetry*, 27–45. New York: First Vintage Contemporaries Edition.

Carson, Anne (2008) 'Variations on the Right to Remain Silent', *A Public Space* 7: 174-87.

Cuomo, Joseph (2010) 'A Converstaion with W. G. Sebald', in Schwartz, Lynne (ed.) *The Emergence of Memory: Conversations with W. G. Sebald*, pp. 93-117. New York: Seven Stories Press.

D'Agata, John (2003) *The Next American Essay.* Saint Paul, MN: Graywolf Press.

Davis, Lydia (1998) *Almost No Memory.* New York: Picador.

Patience (After Sebald) (2012) Grant Gee (director).

Glass, Ira (2012) 'Retraction', *This American Life* (460). Chicago: Public Radio International.

Hejinian, Lyn (2000) *The Language of Inquiry.* Berkeley, CA: University of California Press.

Shengold, Nina (2007) 'Little Miracles', *Poets & Writers Magazine* (July/August): 36–41.

Marr, Andrew (2012) *David Hockney: The Art of Seeing – A Culture Show Special* (21/31) BBC2, 27 February.

McDonald, Jennifer B. (26 February 2012) 'In the Details' in *The New York Times Sunday Book Review,* www.nytimes.com, accessed March 2012, http://www.nytimes.com/2012/02/26/books/review/the-lifespan-of-a-fact-by-john-dagata-and-jim-fingal.html?pagewanted=all accessed 14032012

Perry, Grayson (2011) *The Tomb of the Unknown Craftsman.* London: British Museum.

Reeder, Elizabeth (2010) 'between places: if, then, essay', *PN Review 196,* 38–40.

Reeder, Elizabeth (2009) 'Ramshackle, a novel, and microbursts and topologies, lyrical essays', *PhD Thesis.* Glasgow: University of Glasgow.

Tempest Williams, Terry (2001) *Refuge: An Unnatural History of Family and Place.* New York: Vintage Books.

Woolf, Virginia (1937) 'Words Fail Me', *The New Yorker,* www.newyorker.com, accessed March 2012, http://www.newyorker.com/online/blogs/books/2009/08/virginia-woolf-words-fail-me.html

INDEX